ISLAM, THE WEST AND THE WORLD

Copyright © 2022 Musa Damao

All rights reserved.

Cover Design by Musa Damao

First Publisher:
LAP Lambert Academic Publishing

All rights reserved. No part of this work or publication may be reproduced, stored in a retrieval system, or transmitted, in any form or by any means, electronic, mechanical or photocopying without the prior permission of the copyright holder.

Any trademark, service marks and product names are presumed to be the property of their respective owners and are used only for reference. There is no implied endorsement if one of these terms is used here.

To My Father and Mother,
My Wife Norhoda, Datu Hassan and Bai Al-Tahirah,
You mean the world to me!

ISLAM, THE WEST AND THE WORLD
The Shifting Sands of Global Politics from Prophetic Era to Post-American World

Musa Damao, PhD

Contents

Abbreviations   6
Glossary of Arabic Terms   9
Preface   12
Part One   I   **The Rise of Islam**   **14**
Chapter One . . . Just the Facts   15
Chapter Two . . . Empires before Islam   26
Chapter Three . . . The Rise of Muslim Empires   31
Part Two   I   **The Euro-centric World Order 49**
Chapter Four . . . The Rise of Europe in the Global Stage 50
Chapter Five . . . The Shifting Sands of Expansionism 58
Chapter Six . . . America as the Superpower   75
Part Three   I **The Symptoms of the Sick Empire 82**
Chapter Seven . . . The Signs of the Imminent American Collapse   83
Part Four   I   **The Post-American World**   **149**
Chapter Eight . . . Liberal Capitalism on Declining Trajectory 150
Chapter Nine . . . The Great Reset   165
Chapter Ten . . . The Rise of the Digital World 175
Chapter Eleven . . . The Sunset of Petrodollars and the Sunrise of Electronic Money   180
Chapter Twelve . . .The Future Prospects and Challenges 191
Endnotes   206
Bibliography   266
Acknowledgment   275
About the Author   276

Abbreviations

AIIB	Asian Investment and Infrastructure Bank
AKP	Adalet ve Kalkinma Partisi
AS	Alayhi Salam
BARMM	Bangsamoro Autonomous Region in Muslim Mindanao
BRI	Belt and Road Initiatives
BRICS	Brazil, Russia, India, China and South Africa
CAB	Comprehensive Agreement on the Bangsamoro
CAR	Central African Republic
CE	Common Era
CIA	Central Intelligence Agency
COVID-19	Corona Virus Disease 2019
CPC	Communist Party of China
CSTO	Collective Security Treaty Organization
EU	European Union
EV	Electric Vehicle
GCC	Gulf Cooperation Council
GDP	*Gross National Product*
GNA	Government of National Accord
GNC	General National Congress
GPH	Government of the Philippines
IA	Information Age
ICJ	International Court of Justice
ICT	Information and Communication Technologies
IC	Intercultural Communication

ILO	International Labor Organization
IMF	International Monetary Fund
IRGC	Iran Revolutionary Guard Corps
ISIS	Islamic State of Iraq and Syria
LNG	Liquefied Natural Gas
KAG	Kurdistan Autonomous Government
MB	Muslim Brotherhood
MBS	Muhammad Bin Salman
MBZ	Mohammed Bin Zayed
MILF	Moro Islamic Liberation Front
MINT	*Mexico-Indonesia-Nigeria and Turkey*
MNLF	Moro National Liberation Front
NATO	North Atlantic Treaty Organization
NTC	National Transition Council
OIC	Organization of Islamic Cooperation
PCA	Permanent Court of Arbitration
PKK	Partiya Karkêr Kurdistanê
PLO	Palestinian Liberation Organization
RSD	Right to Self-Determination
SAP	Structural Adjustment Programs
SAW	Sallalahu Alayhi Wasallam
SCO	Shanghai Cooperation Organization
SDF	Syrian Democratic Forces
SEATO	South East Asia Treaty Organization
UAE	United Arab Emirates
UN	United Nations
UNEP	United Nations Environment Programme
UNESCO	United Nations Educational Scientific and Cultural Organization
USA	United States of America
WB	World Bank

WEF	World Economic Forum
WWI	World War I
WWII	World War II
XUAR	Xinjiang Uyghur Autonomous Region
YPG	Yekineyen Parastina Gel

Glossary of Arabic Terms

Alayhi Salam	(lit.) Peace Be Upon Him; (fig.) to be pronounced after mentioning the names of all Prophets
Al-Qaeda	(lit.) the foundation; (fig.) Islamist movement organized by Osama Bin Laden
Al-Quran	(lit.) recitation: (fig.) the noble book of Muslims
Assabiyyah	Social Cohesion
Ayatollah	(lit.) sign of Allah; (fig.) title of Shia Scholars
Dajjal	(lit.) Anti-Christ; (fig.) the lying deceiver
Constantiniyya	Constantinople/Istanbul
Imam	(lit.) Leader
Khawarij	(lit.)The ones who secede; (fig.) the ones who separated from the ranks of Caliph Ali
Khilafa Rashida	Rightly Guided Caliphate
Madina	(lit.) City: (fig.) the City of the Prophet
Makkah	The birthplace of Islam
Mamluk	(pl. Mamalik) (lit.) non-Arab slaves; (fig.) Slaves who established an empire in Egypt
Masih	The epithet of Prophet Isa (Jesus Christ)

Mujahideen Combatants	(lit.) volunteers for Jihad; (fig.)
Muqaddimah	(lit.) Introduction; (fig.) book of Ibn Khaldun
Muslim	Islamic believer
Nabi	Prophet
Sahaba	(pl. Ashab) (sahabas: Anglicized) companions of the Prophet
Salafi	one who wishes to follow the righteous predecessors
Sallalahu Alayhi Wasallam	(lit.) Peace and blessings be upon him; (fig.) exclusively attached to Prophet Muhamad's name
Sham	Greater Syria
Shia	(lit.) group; (fig.) it came from the Arabic term Shiatu Ali mean "the faction of Ali."
Sultan	(lit.) ruler; (fig.) title of the leader of Ottoman Empire
Sunni	(lit.) follower of Sunna or tradition of the Prophet
Takbir	(lit.) saying Allahu Akbar
Taliban	(lit.) students; (fig.) the group governing Afghanistan
Tasbih	(lit.) saying Subhanallah
Ummah	Muslim nation

Wahhabi	The follower of Muhammad Bin Abdulwahab who follows the strict version of Islam
Wilaya Al-Faqih	(fig.) the political system of Iran where religious scholars govern the country
Zakat	alms; the third pillar of Islam

Preface

The purpose of this book is to analyze different events that happened from prophetic era down to the post-American world. The central thesis of the book is that the rise and fall of several Muslim empires and the advent of United States of America in postwar era are manifestations of an endless power rivalry in world history. It also discloses an important moment in history when the world is governed by one country – this is called the US unipolar moment. How America effectively displaced all former colonial lords in the age of colonialism is an intriguing chapter of world history. This book analyzes the unfolding events especially this time when the world witnesses the return of Great Powers friction. The arrival of the coronavirus has been seen as crossroad of human history. The COVID-19 facilitated the shift of power concentration from a sole superpower to a number of Major Powers. China and Russia challenged the unipolar world order. Turkey, Iran, Pakistan, India and even Venezuela have been challenging the unipolar world order.

There are four parts of the book: Part one – The rise of Islam, Part two – The Euro-centric World Order, Part three – The Symptoms of the Sick Empire and Part Four – The Post-American World.

In part one, the author reviews the different empires before the emergence of Islam and the rise of Islam in the international stage. The second part discusses the rise of Europe and its eventual takeover of the world through colonization. The whole world was at the mercy of Europe during colonial age. Part three highlights the symptoms or warning signs of the imminent collapse of the existing superpower. The fourth part describes the possible situation in post-American world, that is, after the collapse of the existing international system.

In addition to western literatures, I have dissected and carefully reviewed varied Middle East sources and publication of various organizations and websites.

February 2022   The Author

Part One

The Rise of Islam

"The Islamic teachings have left great traditions for equitable and gentle dealings and behaviour, and inspire people with nobility and tolerance. These are human teachings of the highest order and at the same time practicable. These teachings brought into existence a society in which hard-heartedness and collective oppression and injustice were the least as compared with all other societies preceding it....Islam is replete with gentleness, courtesy, and fraternity."
--H.G. Wells

Chapter One

Just the Facts

Social Cohesion is an idea of social solidarity and community's commonality with an emphasis on group consciousness and sense of shared purpose. Ibn Khaldun in his *Muqaddimah* argued that "*assabiyyah*" is a cyclical and directly related to the rise and fall of civilizations: it is strong at the start of a civilization, declines as the civilization advances and then another more compelling assabiyyah eventually takes its place to help establish a different civilization. He also made clear that dynasties have a life span like individuals.[1] That means end will eventually come. Leaders come but they go at an appointed time. Civilization ends when there are corruption, moral degeneration and injustice. Corruption gives birth to internal conflict and therefore people stage uprisings to change the existing order; the social cohesion would eventually lose. The people in the community who are willing to struggle become united. They are ready to sacrifice and brave the challenges. They become powerful in resisting the authorities. This group of people would defeat the urban-dwellers who have less cohesion. They would take over the government and eventually rule.

Islam is the final Divine religion – after Christianity and Judaism – sent to the world for the guidance of mankind. It teaches generosity, justice and love. It is a total submission and surrender to the will of God. It is an entity that bundles the whole world into a bouquet of homogeneous religious community called *Ummah*. Muslims around the world are all brothers enjoying equal rights; Arabs are not superior to Iranians, to Kurds, to Filipinos or to Americans. Islam, as diametrically opposed to the innuendos of its critics, would explicitly mean a religion of peace and tolerance. Islamic civilization is the conduit of previous civilizations – e.g. Babylonian, Chaldean, Greek, Roman, Persian among others – and the western civilization. Today, the pole of power is in western world casting its shadows upon all corners of the world. Islam preaches the gospel of tolerance and mercy. It forbids sort of harum-scarum injustice, debauchery, licentiousness and intolerance. It denounces terrorism, violent extremism and hard line fanaticism and radicalism. Muslims are commanded to be peaceful at all times. In place of "Clash of Civilizations" thesis advanced by Prof. Samuel Huntington[2] and "The End of History" by Francis Fukuyama[3] casting aspersions on Islam, Mohammad Khatami[4] proposed a "Dialogue of Civilizations." The efforts of those who sought to prevent what they feared was an impending clash culminated in the fall of 1998 with UN member states declaring the year 2001 as the "UN Year of Dialogue among Civilizations." 'Dialogue among civilizations is an absolute imperative' said Iranian President Khatami (1997–2005), one of the major players behind the proposal. Contextualizing the need for dialogue in the process of globalization and increase in peoples' awareness of their differences in present-day world politics,

Khatami offered the UN initiative as an attempt to lessen the efficacy of the clash thesis in shaping policy.[5] In the contemporary world, initiating dialogue to promote understanding is on the cards especially in the international arena aiming to jointly end the notion of separatism and exclusivism among religions. Interreligious dialogue is of paramount to defy the threat of "*takfirism*."[6] To put it in other way, dialogue is a key antidote against the sweeping ideological spread of bogus caliphate system headed by extremist groups. Militant face of Islam after the emergence of Taliban[7], Al-Qaeda[8], Boko Haram[9], Al-Shabab[10] and Islamic State of Iraq and Syria (ISIS)[11] has been at most highlighted in lieu of its tolerant and caring face. In reality, Islam is not as black as it is painted. Coexistence and religious tolerance have been seen as time-honored trademark of Islam from its early history beginning fourteenth centuries ago.

In the Quran, Allah says:

> "Call to the way of your Lord with wisdom and fair admonition, and argue with them in the kindest way. Your Lord knows best who is misguided from His way. And He knows best who are guided."[12]

There is no compulsion in religion. No one is forced to be converted. "Compulsion and force conversion" has no place in Islam. Dialogue is the best way to deal with the differences. Historically, Prophet Muhammad, Sallalahu Alayhi Wasallam (SAW) all through his life had shown Islam's forgiving and giving face to people regardless of their religions, beliefs, races, lineages and statuses in life. His Makkan life vividly showcased a kind of man who could live in the midst of oligarchs and oppressors without lifting his finger to vendetta. Until such moment that situation was unbearable that they needed to migrate to Madina. Later, he was enthroned by people in the pulpit of leadership. Madina was then a mixed and heterogeneous society composed of Jews, non-Jews and a pocket of Christians. Given that he was the leader and the power was certainly in his hands, constitution was at his behest. Consequently, he requested the scribes to write the "Constitution of Madina" as a law governing the people. He did not impose Quran as a law because there were non-Muslims in

Madina. The constitution assured the primacy of equal security, legal and other rights of the people.[13]

Stephen Schwartz postulated that based on the constitution of Madina, one and all was free to hold fast to any belief or to make any political or philosophical choice. People sharing the identical views could come together and form a community. Everyone was free to exercise his own justice system. However, anyone who committed a crime would be protected by no one. The parties to the contract would engage in cooperation with one another, endow with support for each other, and would still remain under the asylum of Prophet Muhammad. Conflicts between and among the parties would be brought to the Messenger of God. This contract was in full force from 622 to 632 CE. Through this document, the tribal structures which had formerly been based on blood and kinship were abolished and people of different cultural, tribal and geographical backgrounds came together and formed a social unity. The Constitution of Madina secured absolute religious freedom.[14]

The second Caliph, Omar Bin Khattab, exhibited tolerant form of Islam when he captured Jerusalem. When the Muslims opened Jerusalem, it was an enclave of Christianity. Bishops were in sorry; they were afraid that they would be killed unpityingly. Contrary to their conjecture, the caliph did not demolish their church or force them to embrace Islam; what they witnessed was such an amazing clemency of the victors upon their

---

subjugated enemy. The church remained standing. Then, caliph prayed outside the church. The bishop could not believe such kind of humane and tolerant attitude.

Islam showed its tolerance when Salahudin Al-Ayyubi (Anglicized, Saladin) defeated the crusaders and recaptured Jerusalem. Previously, Crusaders when they conquered Jerusalem, they massacred the people and pillaged the city. Instead of revenge, Saladin did not lift his finger and mass murder the Christians. They were freed and returned back to Europe while other Christians remained in Jerusalem. The banner of Islam was hoisted while Churches and temples rebuilt and renovated. He pardoned the vanquished Christians. The foregoing tolerant chronicle explicitly portrayed the canvas of Islam as a peaceful religion.

Furthermore, one of the most debated verses reads, *"Believers, take neither Jews nor Christians for your friends. They are friends with one another. Whoever of you seeks their friendship shall become one of their numbers"*.[15] This has been interpreted by extremists as corroborating separatism, isolationism and the rebuff of mixed communities, while being taken by Islamophobes as evidence that Muhammad's followers look at non-Muslims as cold-hearted enemies. Such claims are belied by the history of Islam. If Muhammad had been separatist and Islam is extremist religion, as imagined by today's extremist e.g. ISIS, it would not have become a global religion.

A millennium of Islamic rule in Middle East and the world starting from the prophetic time down to the liquidation of the Ottoman Empire,[16] Christians and Jews have been left safe and unharmed. There are millions of Jews and Christians in Mideast today; they were not harmed and expelled in the past millennium. There were instances that the attending doctors and advisers of Caliphs were Jews and Christians especially in Arab Spain.[17] The Holy Quran stresses the fact that Islam is nonviolent and peaceful religion. Dialogue is imperative and essential. When there is dialogue, understanding and tolerance spring out. In retrospect, Islamic history is stuffed with dialogue. In due course, there is a need to differentiate Arab imperialism and Islam's expansion around the world. The former is the expansion of Arab territory and political influence in eastern and western part of Mideast especially during Umayyad and Abbasid dynasties. Their political, cultural and economic values were not necessarily Islamic. The latter precisely refers to the expansion of Islam largely attributed to its spiritual appeal. For instance, Muslims in Indonesia—which is the largest Muslim country in the world when it comes to population—embraced Islam not because of military conquest but through trade and peaceful preaching.

Unfortunately, it is a time-honored strategy of self-proclaimed leaders, starting in bygone days until now, to utilize religion for their political goal. Religion becomes a capital for vested interests. Power-hungry behemoths have been using religion to establish their empires and nations. Ironically, those who engaged with this business, if you take a look at them, are self-enthroned men of God. You can see them as if they have to annihilate evils on earth in a single moment but the reality is the opposite. The pages of history are full of this kind. One thing is common to all: fanatics and extremists are openly religious, Pharisee-like people. Among their characteristics is that they are too holy in public.

In contrary, the prophet of Islam respected and did not demolish the synagogues, churches and other religious places in Madina when he had the power to do it. Religious extremism appeared much later when civil wars had occurred in the World of Islam. As a matter of fact, in medieval age, Christians and Muslims were fighting each other not because of theological differences but differences of political interests. The untold variables of these various wars in history are expansionism, imperialism and Materialism.

Islam established an empire that was matchless in the history of mankind. Muslims throughout history have been constructing empires one after the other. Arabs conquered large swathes of territory beginning the rule of the four caliphs until the fall of the Abbasid Caliphate.[18] The downfall of Abbasids paved the way to the rise of Turks. They established two powerful Islamic Empires i.e. Seljuk[19] and Ottoman. After the defeat of the Ottomans from the European powers, Europe began the partition of Muslim lands. Muslim Ummah was effectively and systematically defeated. From then on Europe successfully conquered Islamic lands from North Africa to India and from Central Asia to Indonesia. Each Muslim land was occupied by one of the European Powers. The natural resources and raw materials located in the Islamic world were transported to Europe. The world in general was too small to the insatiability of Europe. Great Britain and France divided Africa and the Arab world. Germany claimed North Africa. The unchecked and too much competition of the Great Powers accelerated world wars. The truth is that world wars, i.e. WWI and WWII, were European wars waged against one another. These two world wars expedited the power shift from Europe to America. United States of America (USA) appeared a superpower after Europe was in ruins. After seventy-plus years, America has all the symptoms of a falling empire.

But US has successfully navigated myriad of challenges; since 2001, it has been dragged in an endless and potentially devastating war. In 2008, irreparable economic crisis surfaced in American economy that speeded the closing of banks and the banking system itself was struggling for life. War around the world is not simple; there is a need for king's ransom. Printing dollars ceaselessly is not enough to fund this war. The international system emerged in postwar period brought US to power. The end of the cold war has portended a new vision of the global order. Although Fukuyama's neo-Hegelian theory in his "The End of History" thesis admits the prominence of religious fundamentalism and ethno-nationalism in global politics, he stresses that "western liberalism" will eventually prevail over possible challenges presented by these analogous phenomena.

There is an incontestable argument that American Empire is ending. The conception is not coming from outsiders but from American analysts galore. One important consideration is that there are many American interests that are muscularly blocked by Russia, China and other powers. In addition, America is defeated thrice in Middle East and Asia. First in Afghanistan, US sent her huge military forces plus North Atlantic Treaty Organization[20] (NATO) and the coalition of the willing with cutting edge weapons and state-of-the-art military equipment. However, Taliban with 1960s weapon model were able to fight them. After two decades of combat mission, it was US officials who looked for ways for negotiation. Second in Iraq, US left the country in ruins; it was Iran which groomed this mess. US archenemy is increasingly expanding and becoming powerful in Mideast. Third in Syria, US left the country in destruction. Syria sustained a powerful resistance under the guiding hands of Russia and Iran. The "three defeats" namely Afghanistan, Syria and Iraq are said to be the three open wounds of American empire. Also, a Turkey-US relation is on rock bottom situation, though Turkey suffers from identity crisis. Turkey seems to have the burdens of balancing its inclination between NATO and the Ummah's side.

On opposing side of the narrative is that, in current global structure, US is still the unchallenged superpower by which the majority of the countries are orbiting around its axis of influence. The Arab world is still a pillar of this world order. The Arab League conferences kowtow US decisions. The agenda of Arab conferences are mainly aligned in the interest of Washington. The two American continents are still in the backyard of US that it has to groom from time to time. Europe is still a colony of US. Therefore, there is no potent challenger of the new world order. Russia is militarily powerful but it has no political power. Russia has no ideology that can offer to the world in order to become "alternative" to capitalism[21] if US ideology will collapse. China has no alternative ideology in place of international capitalism. China's "Socialism with Chinese characteristics in the new era", speaks on its own. It is an ideology which could not be an international ideology that the world could enjoy. The assertiveness of China is confined to establishing a "say" in the present world order. This is the other side of the story.

Furthermore, the rise of America in the global stage facilitated the prevalence of democracy, rule of law, equality, justice, liberty and brotherhood in and of humanity. These values sent America to the center of power. After decades of American high position in global stage, these values were abandoned to sate its imperial hubris.

Chapter Two

Empires before Islam

The goal of imperialism is to establish an empire. There are three methods of imperialism: military, economic and cultural.[22] Its basic method is military imperialism. Napoleon Bonaparte, for instance, equipped with the idea of French Revolution chose to establish supremacy in Europe and the world by means of military conquest. He could have used cultural imperialism to spread the notion of French Revolution but to attain his imperialistic goal military conquest is the best way. The nation that starts war for imperialistic end may gain an empire and hold it. The victors can transform and shape international order. This is why nations which want to control the world would always prepare for war.

The world has experienced plethora of wars since the genesis of time. There were wars in the past among empires, nations and kingdoms. There were wars between tribes and sects. There were countless civil wars happened. The history is replete with the narrative of wars. The bottom-line is that wars have always been banging up-to-date because of power and economic competition. The question will occur in our mind asking when will be the end of all wars and when will peace truly reign in the world. Perhaps, answering these questions would be the most trying and difficult undertaking.

War is as old as civilization. Sumerian civilization was established more than 6,000 years ago. It did not last for so long because Akkadians messed Sumerians up. Then it lost in time. Akkadians prevailed and formed an empire. The first empire that had ever appeared on earth is the Akkadian Empire. Akkadians governed Mesopotamia for centuries. It existed not without threat from outside forces. Periodic wars occurred. Then it fell in the hands of Babylonians. Babylonians had wars with Hittites, and then the latter carried the day. Assyrians, then Chaldeans (the new Babylonians) and then Persians established their respective empires. The rise and fall of empires were made possible after series of wars. War is an instrument used for both the rise and fall of empires and kingdoms.

One of the early great wars in history, if not the first most violent one, is between the Greeks and the Persians. In 546 B.C.E., Persian Empire expanded its territory far and wide. Cyrus the Great attacked Lydia in Asia Minor. After his death his son, Darius I continued the offensive against the Greek colonies. None of the Kings met such hardships as Darius even at the beginning of his reign. Despite that, he proved that he was worthy to be the successor of his father. He possessed the features of iron will, self-confidence and resolve. Darius showed bravery and courage to defeat the enemies and to further punish the Athenians by crossing the Aegean Sea. Upon knowing the further offensive, Athens prepared for the forthcoming fierce wars. Then in the end, Athens won the war. Then Xerxes, Darius's son, pursued the conquest but because of the good defense of Athens, he lost the war. After the Persian threat, city-states lost their unity and wars between them ensued. Sparta defeated the Athens in 404 B.C.E.

King Philip of Macedonia desired to unify the city-states of Greece under his imperial rule. He conducted an onslaught against Athens and Thebes. He was victorious. Such was the end of the glory of Athens. His son, Alexander the Great, inherited Macedonian empire. He conquered all the known world of his time. He was successful in his global conquest. Egypt, Persia and India were beaten and vanquished. Persians felt the vengeance of the Europeans. In post-Alexander period, another power emerged in this part of the world: The Roman Empire. The rise and fall of Rome is one of the interesting and amazing chapters of world history. Rome began as a city located near the Tiber River but like others, it became a big empire. During the peak of its power, its borders were Euphrates River in the east; Atlantic Ocean in the west; the rivers of Rhine and Danube in the north and Sahara Desert in the south.

In 330 C.E., Emperor Constantine transferred the capital of Roman Empire in Constantinople (now Istanbul) which was populated by Greek-speaking people. When Rome in Italy became a capital in 395 C.E., it was no longer the capital of the vast and unbroken empire but of western part of the Empire. The eastern part of Roman Empire became the Byzantine Empire. While the distance of the two parts of empire (Western Europe and Eastern Byzantium) became farther and farther each day passing, the cultural and traditional differences were becoming explicit. For instance, Rome was using a Latin language in the church like in mass and sacrament while Constantinople was using Greek language. The Priests in Rome did not grow beard while in Constantinople, they were bearded. The most glaring difference is that the pope of Rome did not have role to play in government while the patriarch of Byzantine was the head of state and religion. The official divorce of Rome and Constantinople was in 1054. The pope sent his emissary to Constantinople to discuss the differences for reconciliation if possible. However, they did not have meeting of minds; they disagreed with each other. The pope of Rome excommunicated the Patriarch of Constantinople and the latter did the same to the former. Their separation was complete and absolute.

Shortly before the advent of Prophet Muhammad, Arabs were disorganized and that they were busy to their respective tribes. There was no central government that managed their daily affairs. They could not think of a possibility of defeating their neighboring powerful empires of Persia and Rome. They felt insignificant and inferior before these two Powers. An Arab by the name of Qatadah introduced the Arabs as most miserable. He said, "The Arabs were caught between two lions, from both of whom they feared."[23]In addition to this sorry situation, when the Prophet invited the Arabs to the fold of Islam, he encountered al-Muthanna ibn Haritha who remarked, "We are caught between two stretches of water. On one side lie the Arab shores; on the other lie Persia and Khosrow rivers. We have pledged to Khosrow not to create any problem and not to protect or shelter any wrongdoer. Perhaps your ideologies are not palatable to the

Kings. If we do anything wrong here, it would be pardoned, but such mistakes and errors in the Persian borders are not pardonable by Khosrow, the King of Persia."[24]

Aside from the two mighty empires, there were also kingdoms which were independent: Ethiopia and Yemen. Yemen was under the leadership of a Jew, Dhu Nuwas. He announced Judaism as the official religion. He suppressed the Christians of Najran who had friendly relations with Ethiopia. The oppression of the Jews had a political color. Yemeni Jews wanted that Ethiopia should not interfere in the internal affairs of Yemen. After the big massacre of Najran's Christians, one of them escaped and beseeched the Ethiopian emperor for help. This was the beginning of war between these two countries. This resulted to the defeat of Dhu Nuwas in 525 C.E. and Najran became a center of Christianity once and for all. Yemen became a colony of Ethiopia. Christians of Yemen led by Abraha, an Ethiopian leader, had attacked Makkah shortly before the birth of the Holy Prophet.

Chapter Three

The Rise of Muslim Empires

Islam came when the two superpowers namely, the Persian and Roman Empires were at each other's throat. This new ideology was able to destroy the civilizations which existed for thousands of years. For millennium, Islam incontrovertibly ruled the world. It conquered the entire known world and it effectively displaced Rome and Persia in what then became Middle East. Kings, Monarchs and dynasties came one after the other ruling the empires that Islam had created. The first government was established in Yathrib where Prophet Muhammad had to serve as the head of state. Yathrib was renamed as Madinat-an Nabi (The City of the Prophet) during his migration. He constructed a city-state with different people living. The population of the state was composed of Christians, Muslims and Jews. They had rules and systems to be followed.

The city-state of Madina was a melting-pot of people. There were Jews and Christians who practiced their own religious and ritual activities. The prophet turned his attention to an important responsibility of establishing friendly and humanitarian relations with other tribes. The prominent Jewish tribes were Banu Qaynuqa, Banu Nazir and Banu Qurayza. The prophet extended friendly overtures. As a leader of Madina, he initiated a new peace treaty with them. This agreement granted full religious freedom to the Jews. All the inhabitants of Madina had to live in peace and good relations together as brothers. After this treaty, Islam found a safe home in Madina.

The Madina government endured various attacks from outsiders. There were numerous wars waged against the Muslims but they effectively sustained the resistance. The biggest battle in Madina is the Battle of the Trench. The enemies and hypocrites assembled a colossal force of twenty-four thousand. This large army is combined forces of internal and external enemies of the prophet. After the prophet came to know the Jewish plot of exterminating Muslims, he consulted his companions. Salman Farsi suggested that a defensive trench be dug around Madina. Three thousand men worked for twenty four days to dig it. The allied forces under the command of Abu Sufyan marched to Madina. They decided to lay siege to the city. After several weeks of the siege, a cyclone hit Madina for three days and nights resulted to the blowing away of their tents. Their foods became unusable due to the rain. Discouraged, the Quraysh abandoned the siege.

The city-state of Madina was able to shake the existing world order. The prophet defended it from powerful enemies for years. He sent letters to the rulers of the world. The companions delivered these letters to Iran, Byzantium, Abyssinia, Egypt and Syria among others. The contents of the letters are the fundamental teachings of Islam. The rulers were invited to accept Islam. Shortly before his death, he dispatched Osama bin Zaid to the territory of the Roman Empire.

After the short period of Madina government, Prophet Muhammad left the world for the Hereafter. Tensions and rivalry dominated the post-prophethood era. People were divided to different factions. One group believed that Prophet Muhammad did not appoint a successor and that the Ummah had to choose leader among them. This group narrated that Caliph Abubakar was unanimously elected as the successor of the prophet in the Saqifa consultation. The primary criteria highly considered were the fact that Caliph Abubakar was his close companion and a long-time friend. While the followers of prophet's cousin Ali believed that he was the rightful leader after the prophet, they did not have options except to follow. They lived under the guardianship of Abubakar for years. Caliph Abubakar pursued the prophet's mission. He dispatched Osama-led military expedition to Syria. He had lots of things to do. He was busy grooming the Muslim society as there were groups which did not recognize him as the leader. As an open defiance, they stopped paying Zakat. This open challenge to the caliph's leadership turned out to be a bloody war. He fought internal wars. It should be remembered that during Abubakar's leadership, wars against peripheral powers were suspended. The conquest in Iraq began during his days but the succeeding Caliph finished it.

Caliph Abubakar appointed Caliph Omar Bin Khattab in his deathbed. Omar succeeded Caliph Abubakar and continued to spread Islam. During Omar's caliphate, Muslims conquered large territories of the two superpowers. He conquered Iraq, Syria, Egypt and Libya. The conquest of Iraq and Syria and the neighboring regions was strategic for Islamic conquest of the world. The victory was sweeping and the dominance of Islam in Arab world and Persia was inevitable. Before he died, he had named a six-man-council to select among them who would become the next caliph. At last, Othman bin Affan was chosen. The spread of Islam was gaining momentum until civil war sparked in the Ummah. Caliph Othman was marred by fatal accusations of nepotism and corruption. Allegedly, he posted his relatives to governorship in different provinces and that there was a widespread corruption. This accusation led to his brutal assassination. After his death, Ali was elected to be the next caliph. His first action was to remove all the governors and changed them with another set of leaders to the indignation of other sahabas loyal to Othman. Other elite Sahabas disagreed over this decision of the fourth caliph.

Civil war took place. The first battle occurred between Caliph Ali and Prophet's wife, Aisha. With senior companions divided, Caliph Ali and Prophet's wife, Aisha, met in Basra (in Iraq) for a military combat. The two forces fought each other so aggressive and ferocious. The brother of Aisha, named Muhammad bin Abubakar, was on Caliph Ali's side. The fight ended when Ali devised a strategy. He commanded Muhammad to catch his sister by the time she falls while Malik Ashtar had to hit Aisha's Camel. When Aisha fell, Muhammad caught her as per instruction. Aisha exclaimed saying, "How dare you touch the body of prophet's wife!" Muhammad whispered, "I am Muhammad, your brother". That was the end of the battle; Aisha went to Makkah and remained silent for the rest of her life. The battle claimed heavy casualties from both sides. The next battle occurred between Caliph Ali and Mu'awiya. The battle of Siffin happened between the two parties. It also claimed more deaths. The war between Kufah (in Iraq) and Damascus lasted for several years and culminated in the martyrdom of Hussein, the Great grandson of the prophet in the hands of Yazid, the son of

Mu'awiya, many years later. The civil war did not end in the Ali-Mu'awiya conflict.

The rebellious people from the ranks of Caliph Ali's forces rebelled against him objecting the negotiation between Ali and Mu'awiya. He had to deal with this group of purists. The biggest war between this group noted in history as "Khawarij" and Ali's group was the battle of Nahrawan. The civil war that ended with Ali's assassination in 661 by Abdur Rahman Ibn Muljiam was a kaleidoscope of warring factions. Caliph Ali tried to negotiate with his enemies in order to keep the Ummah intact, but this only estranged some of his followers.

The death of Caliph Ali marked the end of the "*Khilafa Rashida*" or the rightly guided caliphate. Umayyad grabbed the power in post-caliphate period. Mu'awiya who replaced Caliph Ali was related to Caliph Othman. He had been a governor of Syria after the death of his brother Yazid bin Abu Sufyan who was commissioned to lead the Muslims in Syria during Omar's caliphate. He secured the office of caliphate after the son of Ali, Hassan, agreed not to contest his leadership. Umayyad dynasty founded by Mu'awiya lasted for almost a century. He focused more to internal affairs than continuing the expansion of Muslim territory. After his death, his son Yazid reignited civil war which once and for all featured Ali's partisans and the rebellion of Madina and Makkah. Makkah rebellion was headed by Abdullah bin Zubayr. Yazid perpetrated a number of massacres – one of which was the massacre in Karbala. The Grandson of the prophet and his family were mercilessly killed and butchered.

After the internal fissures, Umayyad Empire continued the war against Europe. At the beginning of 8th century, Tariq Ibn Ziyad invaded Spain without the consent of the Caliph. The Iberian Peninsula was then ruled by Visigoths. Like in Egypt, there was a tension between the ruled and the ruler. By the time, Tariq arrived in Toledo and Cordoba there was no strong resistance. The local populace did not come out to halt the advancing army. In the beginning, defeating Spain was just a footnote for Umayyads. For Muslims, the most important thing was to be ruled not by powerful family but by the most righteous and pious. For the caliph in Damascus, control, order and income carried some weight. Control was maintained by placing governors who collect revenues.

After decades of Umayyad Caliphate, the Abbasid dynasty staged a revolution, organized in distant Khurasan. The victory of the Abbasids shifted the locus of government away from Damascus and toward Iraq. Like Ali's followers, Abbasids believed that Umayyads were not the true heirs to Prophet Muhammad. Abbasids clutched the Islamic empire so hard and they had no intention of relinquishing power they grabbed. The family of Caliph Ali who joined the revolution toppling the Umayyads was cold-shouldered. Like Umayyads, Abbasids suffered from rebellions one after the other. The Seljuk took over the large territory of Abbasid Empire. Back then, the 10th and 11th centuries witnessed the rise of Turkish power. Turkish Seljuk had slowly converted to Islam after that they were hired as mercenaries by the Abbasids. The emergence of the Turkish Seljuk threatened all the established powers in the region. In addition, there were three empires existed in the Muslim world and each leader had to claim to be the rightful caliph. The leader of the Fatimid Empire claimed caliphate while caliph in Arab Spain did the same. The leader of the Abbasid Empire would also take the mantle of caliphate. The Abbasid Empire was declining due to the weight of Ummah it could no longer carry. The Muslim world was in disarray when Mongols came.

The subsequent invasion of the Mongol Empire in 1258 had swept across the Muslim world. Mongols destroyed the Abbasid Caliphate. Mongol's world conquest was destructive and speedy that was never seen before. Armstrong had this to say about the conquest, "The Mongol chieftain Genghis Khan was building a world empire and a clash with Islamdom was inevitable. Unlike the Seljuks, he was able to control and discipline his nomadic hordes, and made them into a fighting machine with a destructive power that the world had never seen before. Any ruler who failed to submit immediately to the Mongol chieftains could expect to see his major cities entirely laid waste and their populations massacred."[25] The Mongol invasion that ruined Baghdad was a severe test. These powerful invaders who bent the knees of sultans, caliphs and imperial leaders had eventually embraced Islam. When they embraced Islam, they established an empire known in history as Mogul empire.[26] This empire was contemporary of the two Muslim empires of Safavid[27] and

Ottoman. If one observes the march of history, there is an irony here. The barbaric Mongols when they became Muslims, they founded a humane, tolerant and pluralist empire. Look at India, they governed the entire sub-continent for two centuries but Hindus were treated with justice and fairness. The evidence is that all through the Mogul imperial rule, Hindu remained Hindu, there was no forced conversion. There were no ethnic-cleansing, empire-sponsored killings and mass murders. This was the reality until European colonialism destroyed this order and the Mogul Empire joined the perished nations.

The coming of the Ottomans in 15th century rejuvenated the Muslim world and thousands of miles away, the Mogul, another Muslim dynasty, expanded south. Ottoman Empire dipped its hands in the politics of Europe. Europe was cross-hatched with divisions between Protestants and Catholics and between two families: Habsburgs and Valois. Habsburgs controlled Spain and under Charles V ruled central Europe while the Valois ruled France directly challenging the Habsburgs. Under Francis I, the conflict between the two families became personal. Having conquered Hungarians, Sultan Suleyman of Ottoman Empire came face to face with Habsburgs. Watching from Paris, Francis I offered friendship and amity to Suleyman. Suleyman seeing the strategic advantage agreed to Francis' offer of alliance. The friendship and alliance of the two remained solid and unbreakable while the two were still alive. French and Ottomans worked very closely to humble Habsburgs. The French alliance was the cornerstone of Ottomans' European diplomacy. The death of Suleyman did not remove Ottomans as a threat to Europe. In 1683, another sultan rose to power and continued attacks in Europe. He came very close to taking the heart of Europe but he was not able to make it because of so many factors. But granting that Ottomans captured Vienna, it would have been difficult to overrun Europe because Russia had become a daunting enemy like the French and English. While Europe was slowly becoming powerful in international stage, the Ottomans were losing their competitive edge. After 1683, Europe started to push back, and the balance tipped. In the first quarter of the 20th century, the Ottomans existed no more.

Islamic Ummah and the Colonization

In a marvelous turning point of history, the rise of Islam was expected by the world. The emergence of Islam in the scene was practically not easy. It grew from a trouble region of the world. Successively, Muslims started to expand their territories. They became prevailing, mighty and powerful. The coming decades were filled with confrontations between Muslims and Persians in the east and Muslims and Romans in the west. Islamic Empire crippled the two former empires, which dominated the world for centuries. Constantinople eventually surrendered to the Muslims in 1453. While Constantinople was falling, the Pope Nicholas V sent his message to Constantine XI, Patriarch of Constantinople, that he could help him reverse the situation provided that the latter would subject to Rome. The Patriarch refused and said that he preferred the Turks to the Latin. That was the real end of the Roman Empire. Those who refused to bow down to the Turks went to Russia.

The western Latin-speaking pope of Rome had been extending his spiritual authority to the so-called barbarian provinces of Gaul and Spain. Pope Gregory the Great converted the Anglo-Saxon invaders of Great Britain. He protected Italy from the ravages of the Franks and Lombards. He was preparing the way that his successor would ultimately crown under his authority the Frankish Charlemagne as the emperor of Rome and the entire west in 800 C.E. Then Holy Roman Empire was born. In the version of western Christianity, there were temporal and spiritual leadership. Temporal leadership was given to the emperor and spiritual to the Pope. While Europe was in crisis, Islam occupied large territories of the world from east to west and from north to south. Muslims reached the gates of Europe on the western part of the globe and they also conquered China and India on the eastern side and even the Far East bowed down to Islam. Muslim traders and merchants carried Islam across Africa and Indian Ocean to Indonesia. In the later part of 16th century, Islam's reach was greater than it ever had been.

Meanwhile, the governments of Europe fought one another instead of invading the world. After 30 years of war between Catholics and Protestants that near destroyed the Central Europe, leaders and rulers gathered in Westphalia in 1648 and agreed to stop the war. They also agreed not to wage wars over religion. This agreement became the peace of Westphalia. The concept of a secular Nation-State was born.

There are numbers of discussions and debates on what and how "state" contributes to domestic peace and order. Many realists defend the need to have a state that can organize the affairs in a particular society. Morgenthau in his "Politics among Nations" put forward that state is but another name for compulsory organization of society – for the legal order that determines the condition under which society may employ its monopoly of organized violence for the preservation of order and peace.[28]

Others concentrated on the insignificance of state. They opined that state was invented by ruling clique to advance their interests. The gist of state is to continue oppression and that society does not need state to realize equality and justice. State is established as a mechanism to rule the people. According to Lenin in his "The State and Revolution," state is the product and manifestation of the irreconcilability of class antagonisms. To Marx, State is an organ of class domination; an organ of oppression of one class by another; its aim is the creation of order which legalizes and perpetuates this oppression by moderating the collisions between the classes. Moreover, state is only the organization that bourgeois society takes on to support the external conditions of the capitalist mode of production against the encroachment as well of the workers as of individual capitalist. Moreover, it is a capitalist machine, the state of the capitalists; hence its necessity ceases and withers away.[29]

Islam has its own conception of nation and state. The Ummah is translated as nation; Muslims in Madina became one Ummah under the pluralist state of the prophet. Now, all Muslims around the world are considered as one Ummah. All Muslims are equal in the sight of Allah. This was emphasized by the prophet in his last sermon in his final pilgrimage. "Arabs are not superior to non-Arabs and whites are not superior to blacks" is the meat of his sermon. By extension, humans are all equal before God. Prophet being an Arab could not elevate Arabs at the top because the reality is that he often castigated them. Lots of the verses in the Quran have warned them that should they leave Islam, Allah would change them and entrust Islam to others. This became reality after the fall of Abbasid Empire when Turks moved forward and wore the mantle of responsibility. Ottoman Turks held the reins of power and conquered Europe in the name of Islam. This means that the notion of nation-state originated from the agreement of Westphalia is perfectly different from the notion of Ummah. In fact, the prophet warned his followers of the impending divisions of the Muslim world into different nation-states.

If one looks at the situation today, he will see a surprising fulfillment of the prediction. The prediction of the Prophet that this Ummah would be divided into seventy-three groups has actually happened. The rise of nation-states in the Ummah has divided the Muslims. The territory became sacred to a tiny Muslim state and that the border turned out to be a wall that an Arab Muslim needs a visa to cross an imaginary line separating his place with that of a Muslim Turk. Worse, these fictional and invented borders were drawn by colonial powers in 1916. The fifty-seven Muslim states on earth have written their own national policies, principles and laws which are opposed to Islamic laws. Their foreign and domestic policies run contrary to

Islam. The present Middle East political wrestling among Muslim states highlights the inviolability of nation-state system.

In post-Islamic world, Muslims suffered from European colonialism. There are two among many Muslim nations which suffered much: Kashmir and Bangsamoro. Kashmir has been suffering from neo-colonial scepter of India. For decades in post-independence period, it did not see peace and that it becomes a buffer zone of the two competing powers of Asia: India and Pakistan. Colonial lords had divided the world including India. Iberian rulers (Spanish and Portuguese) contested India. In order to reach India without passing through the Muslims' territories in the then Middle East, Columbus went to India via Atlantic seafaring. Unfortunately, he reached what then America instead of India. Therefore, he called the people there Indians thinking it was India. In the end, cunning British colonialist held India tightly. It was the most important asset of British Empire. Great Britain guarded India and controlled other colonial powers from entering India. Suez Canal in Egypt was constructed for the sole purpose of making it a short-cut waterway to reach India easily and quickly. Afghanistan was colonized by Britain to make it as a wall to prevent Russia from entering India. In 1947, British granted the independence of Hindu India and Muslim Pakistan. Probably, it was a gift because millions of Muslim and Hindu Indians were used by British power during First World War. It was followed by ensuing civil wars between the two newly-independent states. The eventual partition of sub-continent into two separate states led to the question of Kashmir status.

Kashmir is geographically located between India and Pakistan. Each one of these countries claims a possession of Kashmir. It is Muslim-dominated state. There is India-administered Kashmir and Pakistan-dominated Kashmir as well. However, the large part of Kashmir is under the government of India. Like many other peoples on the continent of Asia, Kashmiris spend the second half of 20th century in a state of war and conflict. The main reason why there has been no peace and stability for fifty years is the oppression of the occupying Indian administration. The Kashmiris wished to resist and fight the oppressive Indian rule and gain their independence. Indian forces carried out three major massacres in the country, in 1947, 1965 and 1971. Tens of thousands of Kashmiris were killed. Neo-colonial state of India has committed unspeakable atrocities against the Kashmiri Muslims. Their houses, mosques and properties were put to ruins.

The autonomous government of Kashmir does not have any power to exercise its self-rule as it is under constant surveillance. Modi-led BJP is an anti-Muslim and a fascist party. BJP-led India puts Kashmiris in hell-like atmosphere. Thanks to the rise of Imran Khan, while speaking in the parliament he had said that any attempt of India to cross the line would have consequences. It was proved true when the Pakistani forces caught and detained the Indian Pilots who flew beyond the lines. This strong position of Prime Minister Khan did not go unanswered from Modi. Prime Minister Modi responded by saying that Imran Khan could not scare the 1.3 billion Indians. This warning of India was followed by the revocation of Kashmiri Autonomy. The situation in Kashmir is delicate, chancy and disastrous. These two powers in Asia have their nuclear weapons that will potentially finish each other.

Colonial masters drew the global borderlines. The former Prime Minister of Great Britain, Churchill, once proudly said that he had drawn the map of Jordan in an afternoon. They drew the present boundaries of all the nations to divide, control and distribute the natural resources among themselves. Global natural resources were deemed spoils of war. In African continent, the result of this remaking of nations was endless conflict between and among tribes and clans – even in the present. When the colonial warlords created the nations in Africa, they blended and melded the people. The former neighbors with close connection culturally were separated while those who were distant from one another suddenly became neighbors. This has a gargantuan impact on nation-building. Then they were given independence. The notion is that it was a raw and fake independence because the indirect motive is that they had to be necessarily in need of masters who would groom them forever.[30] In Bangsamoro, the legacy of colonialism is indisputably piercing, painful and excruciating.

.

The doctrine of "Manifest Destiny" which expedited the banning of Europe to trespass the western hemisphere brought out the idea that United States expansion in American continents was inevitable. Manifest destiny is defined as the notion of American exceptionalism, that is, the belief that America occupies a special place among the countries of the world. The Protestants came to America in 1630 believing that their survival in the new world would be a sign of God's consent. They migrated to America because of religious wars between the Catholics and Protestants. With the Catholics dominating in Europe, Protestants looked for a new place to flourish and perpetuate itself. Besides, the ideology of manifest destiny continued through the 18th century as victorious America won independence from Great Britain, an event that many occasioned to be predetermined and lauded by God and an example of American exceptionalism. Many scholars would say and interpret that America is the last bastion of the true followers of Christ. Evangelicalism was born in America with a belief that before the second-coming, the Holy Israel should be restored. This is the primary reason why America is so busy protecting Israel.

The rising US was at the helm of Americas, Guam and the Philippines. Philippines during the arrival of US had two distinct people; Andres Bonifacio and Emilio Aguinaldo discerned very well that Muslims in the South were distinct and separate people. Among other reasons, US established the Moro Province because she treated Moro as different from the people of North. Unfortunately, as a colonial pattern, US had to blend and mix the two discrete groups of people for obvious reason mentioned above. In the language of President Duterte, this is called historical injustice committed against the Bangsamoro. It is in the crossroad of world history that Bangsamoro nationalism is emerging. In the age of the reemergence of Great Powers rivalry, the Bangsamoro is reasserting its Right to Self-Determination (RSD).

For four decades, the Moro have been asserting their right to be recognized as a distinct people. They initiated several liberation movements to be able to exercise their right to self-determination. They worked for this right through armed struggle and later, they shifted to a more civilized and diplomatic means—a negotiated political settlement of the Moro people—to show the world that their struggle to self-governance is a legitimate one. There have been many peace initiatives undertaken in resolving the conflict in Mindanao. In recent years, peace negotiations were conducted between the government of the Philippines and the two Moro liberation movements/fronts, namely the Moro National Liberation Front (MNLF) and the Moro Islamic Liberation Front (MILF) aimed at resolving the armed insurgency in Mindanao. The MNLF and GPH signed the so-called Final Peace Agreement in 1996 and on March 27, 2014, the MILF and the GPH signed the Comprehensive Agreement on the Bangsamoro (CAB).[31] The Philippine Government and the MILF had reached an agreement which accelerated the establishment of the Bangsamoro Autonomous Region in Muslim Mindanao (BARMM) in 2019.

Part Two

The Euro-Centric World Order

"The West won the world not by the superiority of its ideas or values or religion but rather by its superiority in applying organized violence. Westerners often forget this fact, non-Westerners never do."

-- Samuel P. Huntington

Chapter Four

The Rise of Europe in the Global Stage

During the Middle Ages,[32] the powers of Pope and Emperor were irrefutably vast. There was no freedom. It was such reason that intellectual rebellion against the church became the order of the day. This rebellion facilitated the rise of humanism, secularism and then liberalism. French Revolution[33] was launched that reshaped the European order and the world. The western church was completely defeated and the birthing of new secular order dawned. Philosophers and thinkers revolutionized politics and society. It led to the formation of secular political system. The secular thoughts including the revival of democracy, separation of powers, rule of law, human rights, liberty and absolute freedom among others described the coming world. The church was in retreat and its role in society was removed. Separation of state and religion became the mantra of world powers. Europe, especially France and Great Britain, had a civilizing mission of secularization of the world. The French revolution embodied the end of a social order based on God and King. Intellectuals looked to a new world where reason and science would trump religion.

European renaissance or rebirth was developed after Islam introduced knowledge to Europeans when they were ignorant.

For example, Harun Al-rashid[34] of Abbasid caliphate sent to Emperor Charlemagne a clock, made by his horologists, striking a bell every hour, to the great wonder and delight of the whole court of the newly crowned Holy Roman Emperor.[35] Paper was made known to Europe via crusades. In pre-crusade Europe, Europeans did not know paper. They were astounded by this advanced technology. The crusaders when they returned home, they took hold of paper and studied how to manufacture it. In Andalusia, a Muslim Spain had this already and then after re-conquest they captured Muslims who knew how to manufacture it. Those handfuls of Muslims were able to teach Europeans to put up industrial manufacturing mill to produce paper. There started unbelievable European civilization when they produced philosophers, scientists, educators etc. Gutenberg printing press was presented for the first time. Europeans developed paper which would be better than the one made by Muslims when it comes to quality and quantity. Truly, by means of paper, they could write and read. Knowledge would flow. Books were written and published. Consequently, the barrier between the elites and the commons were removed because everyone could have an access to books. Moreover, the philosophers and thinkers who toppled monarchy in Europe were common people who had learned different sciences brought about by the industry of paper. This time, Islam was on falling course.

After the discovery of printing press, bulk of books flooded Europe. When printed copy of book was seen in the Muslim world for the first time, they prohibited it especially Sultan Salem because allegedly it was against religion and that it was an invention. Once one was found to have printed books would be beheaded. It was then Napoleon Bonaparte who brought printed books in Egypt forcibly. Printing press was for the first time introduced to the Muslims. Paper introduced by Islam is one of the pieces of evidence that it has contributed to the rise of the western civilization.

European Countries were fighting one another. Princes and Kings of different Kingdoms were in conflict. It was this time when Pope Urban II declared war before the bishops and European princes with the aim to liberate Jerusalem from the infidels and aliens who had allegedly desecrated the land which was purged by the pure blood of Jesus. He was able to brainwash and galvanize the European Christian rulers to believing in the existence of an imaginary enemy – to which the knights of Europe were eager to combat with. The idea among other things is that it was a strategy to create a war outside Europe to unify the competing Christian rulers then fight the common enemy. The ensuing circumstance is that Europe arose in global stage as the rising power.

The crusaders were victorious because their arrival was well-timed and opportune. There was no potent resistance. The Muslims were weakened and debilitated by civil wars between the Seljuk Empire and Fatimid Dynasty.[36] Fatimid subjugated the holy land and then the Seljuks were driven away. Interestingly, Seljuks were former soldiers of Abbasids who revolted against them. They betrayed the caliph of Baghdad. They established their own dynasty and government. While Seljuks and Byzantine were busy pitting against each other on one side and Fatimid and Seljuk on the other, Crusaders came in. In addition, the Seljuk underwent division of leadership that had provoked infightings. Each prince had his subjects. Knowing all this drama, Fatimid which was governing Jerusalem, extended their message of friendship to the invading crusaders knowing that they would just end their pillage in Syria. Unfortunately, the primary mission was Jerusalem. Crusaders proceeded to Jerusalem. The weak and war-weary Fatimid who just liberated Jerusalem from Turkish Seljuk did not sustain the war. In the end, Holy Land was conquered by crusaders. The fall of Jerusalem was inexorable.

Middle East saw Arab empire-building for hundreds of years. Arabs arrived at the gates of France after they overran the entire Iberian Peninsula. For eight centuries, Arabs governed and ruled Spain. Then Seljuk Empire held the reins of power in Mideast and afterwards it was humbled by Crusaders and Fatimids. After hundreds of years, Ottomans came and performed their role in this stage play. Ottoman Empire ruled North Africa, Asia and Europe during the summit of its power. It sits in the midst of the three continents. Mediterranean Sea was controlled and policed by ottomans. The Europe carefully treated ottomans with respect. But when Europe garnered power and disunity in the Muslim world emerged, the tide began to turn. Europe began to pillage the possessions of the empire and then Europe managed to divide the whole ottoman territories.

In the last quarter of 1870s Jamal Ad-Din Al-Afghani of Afghanistan sent a letter to Sultan Abdulhamid of Turkey describing the plight of the Muslim world. He recommended to the sultan to use his power and influence to establish a pan-Islamic front against the west. His letter was filled with indignation and anger over the embarrassment of Muslim countries by western powers, thus:

> "When I considered the condition of the Islamic people, it rent the shirt of my patience and I was overcome by fearful thoughts and visions from every side. Like a fearfully obsessed man day and night, from beginning to end, I have thought of these affairs, and have made the means of reform and salvation of this millah my profession and incantation."[37]

Al-Afghani invited the Ummah to organize a strong resistance against the west in order to remove it from the humiliation it was in. He traveled Muslim lands calling for Ummatic reform and transformation. The power of Europe was on its peak while Ottoman Empire was on collapsing track. The Arab world and Persia along with other countries had been on the grip of the western world. Without the pan-Islamic resistance, the Islamic world was falling irreversibly. The main reason why Afghani extended his invitation to the Ottoman Sultan to create a world-wide solidarity among Ummah to defy the encroaching west is that Istanbul was a center of power. Indian Muslims were under constant harassment by British and Muslim Tatars ill-treated by Russians. He was indirectly telling him that the only man who could defuse the situation was Sultan of Istanbul. The reality is that Europe – or the western world in general – had been conquering Ottoman Empire using ideas. Ottomans were so enthralled with Europe. The advancement of its military and technology was envy to Istanbul. And the dissolution of the Ottoman Empire was facilitated by Turkish government itself. Correctly, the final defeat is the defeat of ideology and beliefs.

There are two crucial points in analyzing the shift and transfer of power from one empire to another: claiming the strategic positions and timing of invasion. This was considered and took into account in the fall of the Muslim world. Sham – or France called it Levant (Now Israel, Lebanon, Syria, Jordan and Palestine) – and Egypt are areas of great battles in history. It is a strategic area and a door to wider world. An ambitious country needs to possess it to claim and secure global leadership. Roman and Persian empires had fought fierce battles in history in this strategic area. Because of the intense rivalry between France and Britain, Napoleon Bonaparte occupied Egypt to block the way of Britain to India, the fulcrum of British Empire. Egypt grew into a theater of war because of Suez Canal. France also used Egypt as center of its imperial ambition. Through Muhammad Ali, Ottoman governor of Egypt, France conquered Lebanon and Syria. He was used by France to finish Istanbul. Seeing the threat of Mamluks in 1811, Muhammad Ali invited all of their leaders to his palace to celebrate the declaration of war against the Wahhabi-Saud alliance in Arabia. Muhammad Ali's forces killed almost 700 Mamluks near the Al-Azab gates in a narrow road down from Mukatam Hill. This ambush came to be known as the Massacre of the Citadel.

Time is a vital element in the shifting of power. Timing is a first consideration in defeating the enemies. Crusaders had easily taken the holy land because of the fact that Muslim defenders were so weary and tired of civil wars. Seljuk and Fatimid empires were drained and exhausted fighting each other. The same is true when Ottomans conquered Constantinople. The timing was so great that the conquest was so easy because the Christian world was disunited. The office of the Pope sent a message to the Emperor of Constantinople stating that the former would be willing to rescue the falling empire if it would bow down to the pope. The Emperor rejected the offer thinking that the Pope was just a Bishop under the office of the Patriarch of Constantinople. Then the emperor replied, "Better the turban of the Muslim in the midst of Constantinople than the miter of the Latin."[38] Later, the empire crumbled, dissolved and gone.

The European powers considered also the timing when they struck and invaded Muslim lands. There were rebellions in the Arab world: Al- Saud[39] of Arabia and Sharif Hussein[40] of Jordan revolts. British Empire used these two important pawns to weaken the Ottoman Empire. The powers made use of the internal squabbles in the Islamic world. In 1916, the present boundaries of Arab countries in the Middle East were drawn. France and Britain divided the region. The once mighty Ottoman Empire shared the fate of the perished nations. In 1917, British Empire awarded Palestine to Jewish people through Balfour declaration. Palestine was governed through British mandate and finally in 1948 Israel was born. Jews around the world were tantalized to go to the Promised Land. There were many initiatives to extract Jews from different countries to finally settle in Palestine.

Chapter Five

The Shifting Sands of Expansionism

When time had come to propagate the life-saving mission of Islam, Muslims tried to penetrate Europe in different times and directions. Firstly, Muslim Army reached the southern part of France in 8th century via Spain. Spain was administered by Visigoths who oppressed their own people. The ruled who struggled from mistreatment of their rulers did not pick their weapons to fight the arriving Arabs. The Arabs overran the entire peninsula. They had pursued sweeping military invasion until they reached France. It was the sustained resistance and strong defense of Franks which fettered the advancing Muslim army. Secondly, Muslim Army got a foothold in Vienna during the peak of Ottoman powers. Ottomans were able to reach the heart of Europe via Constantinople. It was the domestic and internal infightings that halted the victory. It is also noteworthy to consider that Europe had constructed best defenses against the occupying Ottomans. Not long time had passed when Europe was able to colonize every inch of the earth. Later, the history-altering fall of Ottoman Empire unfolded before the eyes of the Ummah. It earned its humiliating title, "the sick man of Europe."

The third direction is in Russia; it is often overlooked by western historians. Mongols conquered East Asia, much of Russia and Eastern Europe. They established a state known as Khanate of the Golden Horde. In the third quarter of 13th century, Berke Khan, the grandson of Genghis Khan and lord of the golden horde, converted to Islam. When they wholeheartedly hugged the values of Islam, they continued their imperial invasion using Islam as ideology. This is widely regarded in the annals of Russia as "The Tatar Yoke." The invading Muslim Mongols brought Russia to its knees. They proceeded to Europe but faced with countless hindrances. When Russia was caught between the two enemies – European Catholic forces and Muslim army – it had the decision to make, either to join the Christians or to choose the Muslims. It opted to join and be a subject to Muslim army. In 1475, the Khans in Crimea became the vassals of Ottomans.

At some points, there was a bitter war between Christian Byzantium and Muslim Abbasid dynasty. They were especially at variance with each other because of rivalry over lands, territory and people. They were neighbor empires – Byzantine Empire was sitting in what is now Istanbul and the Abbasid was in what is now Baghdad. Numerous armed clashes between the two giants were recorded. Another series of wars occurred between the rising Seljuk Turks – the successor of Abbasids – and the Byzantine forces. This intense power contest was not about Christian-Muslim relations in general. The fact is that Christian Byzantine had a diplomatic relation with Muslim Spain. They were natural friends because of their common objective, that is, to remove Abbasids as threat. Also, the two Christian Powers namely Byzantium and Holy Roman Empire were enemies. During the crusades at some point, Crusaders from Europe would pass through Mediterranean Sea to avoid walking in the territory of Byzantium before reaching the holy land. .

Christian Holy Roman Empire of Europe and Muslim Andalusia-Umayyad dynasty were not in good terms with each other. They had been fighting for rather a long time. In contrary, Holy Roman Empire had been a friend to Muslim Abbasid dynasty especially during Emperor Charlemagne while Arab Spain and Baghdad governments were rivals. The ruler of Islamic Spain was crowned as caliph of Ummah so was the Abbasid caliph sitting in Baghdad. Wars between Muslims were not less violent compared to Muslim Army against other religions. The war between various Muslim dynasties was characterized by violence and brutality.

In the past, Islam put the Arabs in the limelight and they were able to establish empires that would last for centuries. They crippled the two superpowers: Persia and Rome. They introduced caliphate system in the literature of world politics. And in 1258, the Arab Abbasid caliphate was devastated by the conquering Mongols. The downfall of the Arabs did not mean the death of Islam. The Turks from central Asia filled the leadership vacuum. The prediction of the prophet and the Quranic warning of changing the Arabs with "Other People" became a reality. The Turks founded a caliphate that would rule the Muslim world, Africa, Mideast and Europe for the next six centuries.

Following the downfall of Granada, Spain and Portugal emerged as Great Powers. When Spain and Portugal had stretched their muscles in search of world's wealth, they employed myriad of strategies. They were rivals in search of the pearls of Orient. The biggest challenge to these rising powers was the Muslim world as they had painful experiences with one another. They could not reach east so easily because they could pass by the Mediterranean world all the way to Arabia before reaching India,

China and finally the East which was the locus of riches. They discovered that East could be reached via West. Mr. Columbus attempted it. So, he planned to go to India via west journey. When he landed America, imagining it was India, he called the native inhabitants, Indians. He lost the way, actually. So, Iberian powers started to set up and occupy the newly-found territory–a new world. The two rivals divided America and the world later. Spain used Mexico as the center of its empire. When US became the Superpower–after it defeated Spanish Crown–she shooed away Spain. After years, Latin America was under the tutelage of US. It became and considered as backyard of US. No powerful country had the audacity to compete with US in relation to Latin America. In cold war era, it was Russia which had tried but failed.

Europe, in its own right, defied the offensive of the Ottoman Empire. The wind of invasion was effectively put to a halt in the gates of Vienna. The end-time prophecy was unfolding that Ummah would suffer a terrible loss. European nations divided the Islamic empires and the rest of the world. British Empire had the big share in this pie. This led to a catastrophic war that would change the world forever. Ottoman Empire could not be defeated if it was cohesive, unified and organized but because of British cunningness and cleverness – to some a form of deception or at least deceptive diplomacy – Arab revolt was staged.

British secured two primary pawns in the Arab world: Sharif Hussein in Jordan and Saud-Wahhabi alliance in Najd. T.E.

Lawrence or popularly known as Lawrence of Arabia[41] was sent to Sharif Hussein to stage Arab revolt against the Ottoman Empire. He was able to successfully perform his part in this stage play. To Ibn Saud, a British military was sent to him. His name was Harry St. John Bridger Philby. He was a former colonial official in India. Through Philby, Ibn Saud had agreed to a treaty with Britain in 1915 making his domain protectorate. He promised, in return for cash and arms, to fight Al-Rashid, the Ottoman governor.

In postwar geopolitical re-arrangement, Britain was in dilemma because it had to choose who would lead the Arab world. Sharif Hussein wanted to revive the caliphate in his own version because it is an Islamic system worth maintaining and sustaining. He did not know that Europe wanted to remove caliphate system because it was the stumbling block to its colonial ambitions. Contrarily, Al Saud family and its Wahhabi ally had no intention of such renewal or revival. They saw a different path. Finally, British took Al Saud and abandoned the main actor of Arab revolt, Sharif Hussein, who later opted to join Russian camp.

In 1926, under British command Ibn Saud called for world Muslim congress informing the Ummah that custodianship of the two holy mosques was awarded to him. And it was renewed when Saudi Arabia became an independent state. British Empire had effectually arranged postwar Mideast. The Mideast regional order shaped by Ottomans collapsed. Modern Israel and Saudi State were born. The state of Israel was proclaimed in 1948. Revolt and protests were staged to thwart the creation of Israel but of no use. The tiny Israel is getting bigger and powerful. What more dramatic than anything people can conceive is the discovery of the oil in Saudi Arabia which changed the tide in world affairs. Saudi Arabia being the pawn in colonial era became the pillar of America in decades. Thanks to the oil, Saudi turned out to be a world power. After the Vietnam War, USA was deeply in crisis. Secretary of State, Kissinger, went to Riyadh for an important meeting. That meeting reshaped the global economy for the betterment of these two world powers. The petro-dollar was introduced to the economic system. This means US could now print dollars in maximum level and the oil could now incessantly flow.

In 19th century or even before, British Empire and the rest of European Powers were busy looking for the glitters of the earth until such time that they were made to fight one another. In prewar period, there were major powers such as France, Germany, Austro-Hungarian Empire, Great Britain, Russia and Ottoman Empire and one dark horse in the Atlantic, the USA. The balancer and the ruling power was Great Britain. Financial center of the world was London and it was in the hands of the Rothschild. Rothschild owned huge banks in Europe. They possessed the banks where major powers had to borrow money especially in funding their war efforts with gargantuan interests.

After WWII, United States became the Superpower. Washington turned out to be the financial capital of the world with US Dollar as the sole global currency reserve. For centuries, the center of world politics is in Europe until world wars chanced to transpire which expedited the rise of America in the center-stage. US-centric world order began while Europe was devastated by wars. It was this time when America took the golden opportunity to manage post-conflict situation. America then colonized Europe for decades. Notably, Europe has no independent policy. It is US which would decide what is good for Europe. America led the postwar reconstruction in Europe. Marshall Plan initiated by United States while the whole Europe was gasping and dying. It saved the life of Europe until it regained its power. The victors of the world wars reconstructed the international system when they met in a conference in San Francisco which later introduced global economic system. The conference's output was the bringing into existence of the Bretton Woods system where America would become the captain of the ship. World Bank and International Monetary Fund institutions became important tools of US foreign policies. The allies appeared victorious in the aftermath of World War II.

Subsequent to the said victory of the allied forces, a new system dominated which was then first-time in contemporary world. This system is known as bipolar system. This continued for almost forty years. The meaning of bipolar system is the existence of unmatched domination of the two superpowers of the west and east: US and Russia. The ever-increasing spreading out and consolidation of the two superpowers forced most of the countries to ally with one of the two blocs. Although, there were ups and downs in the relation of the two superpowers throughout bipolar system, the feature dubbed "cold war" dominated series of their relations.[42] Muhammadi further wrote that in 1980s, one of the superpowers faced fundamental and extensive transformation and change, which not only put a significant halt to its internal structure in a surprising manner but made an impact in the international society. Following this collapse of the eastern bloc, US took advantage of this opportunity to extend and widen its unrivaled power over the entire world. The birth of unipolar system was inevitable in which US is no longer a superpower but a hyperpower. USA is appeared to be unchallenged traveling the world's oceans and policing the entire globe. Pursuant to this conception, Bush Doctrine labeled as New World Order[43] brought to the fore. It was such a bold move. New World Order proposed that United States of America, as the only remaining superpower after the demise of cold war order, is in need of preserving a considerable degree of its military power to employ effective global influence.

_____

The inevitable death of communist Russia paved the way to the rise of unipolar world. United States dominated the international system. In bi-polar order, there were enormous prospects of what would be the immediate international order. Foremost was the Clash of Civilizations thesis. According to Prof. Huntington in which he put forth that the post-cold war world would be dominated by clashes and that eight world civilizations would inevitably clash is intellectually shunned. The three most important reasons of this clash of civilizations, in his opinion, are as follows: the conflict of civilizations is fundamental, religious revivalism is on the rise, existing fault lines between civilizations of today have replaced ideological borders of cold war era.[44] In other words, in post-communist world he saw the rise of Islamic and Confucian civilizations. For his critics, clash of civilizations theory is mind-conditioning to prepare the world of an impending rise of Islam and Confucianism as threat to the western world. He did not actually present a paradigm but an alternative idea justifying the inevitable contradictions after the collapse of bipolar system.

Another theory came after the collapse of bipolar system is Fukuyama's End of History. The end of history discourse highlights the idea that after Communist Russia was torn down by western liberal capitalism. The latter would become the dominant ideology around the world. He predicted that nation-state construct would be replaced by globalization.[45] That means there would be no significant barrier of free market economy. However, a couple of years ago, he swallowed his prediction as China came at the forefront of international stage. China as a nation-state is increasingly becoming power in global arena to be reckoned with.

These two prospects became widely held propositions and alternatives after the world was thrown into the desert of confusion after the death of Soviet Union. But the weakness of these theories is exposed to all. The clash of civilizations and the end of history will go down in history as self-fulfilling predictions. New World Order caught the attention of several theoreticians of American universities and they were requested to defend and justify this notion. Among the important theories emerged was structural realism of Kenneth Waltz. In his work "Theory of International Politics," he came forward and stated that although the distribution of military capabilities at the end of the World War II warranted the cold war competition between Russia and US, at the time when in the mid-1980s the USSR lagged behind in preserving and perpetuating its military capability and unnecessarily withdrew from the scene of competition, America as unrivalled power in the international system will remain as such.[46]

Other international relations experts revealed that among the proposed models of the future following the collapse of bipolar world order, three stood out: Fukuyama's theory in "The End of History and the Last Man", Huntington's prophecy in "The Clash of Civilizations and the Remaking of World Order" and Mearsheimer's analysis in "The Tragedy of Great Power Politics." Each presented a bold, audacious and sweeping vision that struck a chord to certain readers. Each one had prophesied a future of the world. These three theories advanced a shared and common idea of future conflict between the west and the rest. Among the most important feature in those clashes is between US-led western civilization and China which was posited by Mearsheimer.[47] On Fukuyama's followers in his "The End of History and the Last Man" seeking for worldwide democratic victory have commendably seen the realization in post-cold war fissure facilitated by and when communism was effectively displaced and thus ceased to be the competitor of western liberalism. To some degree, the victory of liberalism is seen as fulfilled prophecy during US unipolar moment. Moreover, in post-9/11 attack, came the fulfillment of the clash of civilizations and the remaking of world order. It was opined that Islam and the West would inevitably collide when the former Pope himself dipped his hands in the politics of civilizational conflict. The problem of Huntington's civilizational clashes theory is resolved by the idea of Fukuyama's End of History thesis.

Mearsheimer has been putting forward the future relations of China and the west. In the recent period, we see the collision, at least in economic field, between US and China in so many places. The trade war was popular during President Trump and we also see the continuity of this power struggle especially in South China Sea. As the scholar Robert Gilpin has argued, "Hegemonic Transitions" when a rising power begins to overtake the dominant one have rarely been peaceful. "If the United States is not willing to fight against Chinese hegemony, it will need to foreswear its universalism," Huntington warns—but this would be an unlikely sharp turn away from tradition and triumph. "The greatest danger," he fears, "is that the United States will make no clear choice and stumble into a war with China without considering carefully whether this is in its national interest and without being prepared to wage such a war effectively."[48]

If one takes a look at the three future-of-the-world projections, Russia was demystified as weak that had no future role in the coming global competition. The analyses had completely set aside Russia's resurgence in the future. It was unknown before that Russia would come again and recreate Russian empire. After a decade, Russia came back. Presently, if we analyze and note the present scenario with caution, we will find that the west is completely misreading Russia. Russia under Putin is still militarily preeminent. Putin was able to influence some of the important international situations. He had hands in Libya and Afghanistan. Russian Putin was able to facilitate the negotiation between US and the Taliban. And it was Russia which reversed the tide of war in Syria.

The three models of the future would be seen as fulfilled on one side and a wrong estimate on the other. China is exerting its best effort to finally realize Sino-centric Asia. It wants multipolar system as alternative to US unipolar dominance. Consequently, the conflict still persists. The US soft powers such as Hollywood and dollars are facing fundamental difficulties. Petrodollars are on waning path. The rise of electronic money and e-business will effectively give a fatal blow to dollars. This "mountain of gold" according to hadith is collapsing. Gone are the days when US would just print money to solve its financial problems. The only capital is ink and paper at the expense of dying poor Africans and Asians.

The US-led forces have been waiting for the right time to inflict massively-directed onslaught against China. China has also positioned its naval forces in Spratly Islands. In Russia, NATO forces are right on Russia's door. Russia has its powerful military posture. If this future war occurs, it will reshape global balance and order. Moreover, the Huntingtonian Theory became the important guiding theory in analyzing and understanding the coming conflict in the world. It was theorized in post-Cold War period when the conflict between western liberal capitalism and eastern communism had come to an end. The clash of civilizations thesis defined that the immediate coming world conflict is primarily cultural and religious. In postwar years the American monopoly of atomic bomb gave rise to the idea of American Century, a world dominion based upon unchallengeable American power. At footnote, it was a nightmare of the rising empire of Japan when it was bombed by US. Japanese invasion of Asia was almost complete but because of the atomic bombs dropped, Japan unconditionally surrendered thereby ended her colonial ambitions. After the two decades of 21st century, we can say that America is still holding the scepter of global leadership. There are two opposing views in relation to the existing international political reality. On one hand, American empire is on the cliff of destruction and that another world order will be born. On the other hand, America will still be superpower in this present century.

Ikenberry spoke out that scholars use the term unipolarity to distinguish a system with one extremely capable state from systems with two or more great powers. Unipolarity should also be distinguished from hegemony and empire, terms that refer to political relationships and degrees of influence rather than to distributions of material capability. The adjective unipolar describes something that has a single pole.[49] International relations scholars have long defined a pole as a state that (1) commands an especially large share of the resources or capabilities states can use to achieve their ends and that (2) excels in all the component elements of state capability, conventionally defined as size of population and territory, resource endowment, economic capacity, military might, and organizational-institutional competence. A unipolar system is one whose structure is defined by the fact of only one state meeting these criteria. The underpinnings of the concept are familiar to international relations scholars.[50] United States after the fall of Soviet Union is the only state that meets the criteria of a leading state in the world. It has large areas of influence and resources, population and territory, and economic and military reach. Scholars agreed that after cold war, it was US whose unchallenged power is beyond question would become the only Superpower.

On economic parlance, in relation to US premiership, it is argued that over time these and related institutions came to be cogs in what was loosely defined as the "Washington Consensus," that is the basis upon which the global economy would operate. Neo-liberalism gives more power to private institutions than the state. That means the state cannot absolutely control the market. The fundamentals were a reverence for the market system of exchange and favoritism for deregulation over public controls, the liberalization of trade and the reduction of cross-border barriers, the preeminence of the private sector over state enterprise, and respect for private property and legal mechanisms to insure its protection. The term Washington Consensus was a clear indication of where the seat of power resided, and the values that would define it. Associated institutions meant to capture these principles included the United Nations(UN) and its several off-shoots such as UN Educational, Scientific and Cultural Organization (UNESCO) and the International Labor Organization (ILO), originally formed in 1919 and integrated into the UN in 1946, the International Court of Justice (ICJ), the Permanent Court of Arbitration (PCA), and many other such bodies formed in the post-World War II era to address international issues as the nations of the world converged into what has been defined as "globalization." And finally, we could also add defense-related organizations such as NATO and the relatively short-lived South East Asia Treaty Organization (SEATO), as well as various UN agencies devoted to non-nuclear proliferation.[51] The fact that these postwar institutions are located in US would mean that it has a strong influence on the operation.

The Washington consensus, which is seen as unregulated financial capitalism, has collapsed though globalization still exists but all the indications point to its imminent end. Globalization does not lead to a flat world characterized by increasing integration, cosmopolitan openness and breaking barriers. Rather, Europe and United States are marked by growing inequality and unemployment due to mobile corporations traveling around the world in search of cheaper labor and high profits. After the fall of Berlin Wall, globalization was oversold to the world bringing more accelerated development and progress. But the economic growth in the 1990s has been a sorry one. There is still vivid inequality in the present.

Chapter Six

America as the Superpower

Contemporary America is extraordinarily spellbound by imperial Rome. The Capitol and the best train stations in many ways look Roman. Roman and classical images surface in popular culture at regular but not chance intervals: the big films of the 1950s and 1960s, from Ben Hur (1959) Spartacus (1960) Cleopatra (1964), and the fall of the Roman Empire (1964) were also films of the Cold War, in which the imperial analogy looked very eye-catching. The classical blockbusters then stopped quite suddenly, however, with Vietnam-era doubts. The idea revived with Gladiator (2000), Troy (2004) and Alexander (2004). Classical empires literally speak to us – but they require some interpretation.[52] America possessed both soft and hard power that put its incomparability with the rest of the world.

Although there is something distinct about the American Empire, the United States does what all important empires have done in the past: namely, set the principal rules for those who live within the imperium and punish and reward in equal measure those who either disobey or play by these rules.[53] New World Order architecture with US as the superpower has stayed for decades and unless a strong destabilizing revolution and crisis happened only then that change in the present global order shall occur. According to many American political scientists, America has unique and exceptional role in the world. It has been the torch-bearer of democracy, freedom and liberalism; this is called the American Exceptionalism. A Lincolnian rhetoric is depicting America as "the last best hope of man on earth."[54]

The rise of post-Cold War unipolarity alters America's position with other states. Increased power advantages give the United States more freedom of action. It is easier for Washington to say no to other countries or to go it alone. It can decide alone without consulting other powers. Growing power such as military, economic, and technological also gives the United States more chances to control outcomes around the world. But unipolarity also creates problems of governance. Without bipolar or multipolar competition, it is not clear what disciplines or renders predictable US power.[55] Other countries worry more than in the past about dominance, manipulation, and abandonment. They may not be able to organize a balancing of the alliance of other major powers but they can resist US policies.

The first feature of the shift from bipolarity to unipolarity is that it entails greater power advantages for the lead state. According to Ikenberry, the United States has new latitude for withholding cooperation. The cost of non-agreement is lower for the United States than for other states, so this confers bargaining advantages on the United States. There are also new opportunities for other states to free ride on the American provision of global public goods, particularly security protection and the underwriting of economic openness. Unipolarity, in this sense, is a welcome development for frailer states – to the extent that the United States provides those public goods. But it also opens up a new set of distributive conflicts between the United States and other states.[56] The advantage of Unipolarity is that it favors the absence of war among the great powers and somewhat low levels of competition for prestige or security for two reasons: the leading state's power advantage removes the problem of hegemonic rivalry from world politics, and it reduces the salience and stakes of balance-of-power politics among the major states. This argument is based on two famous realist theories: hegemonic theory and balance-of-power theory. Each is controversial, and the relationship between the two is complex. For the purposes of this analysis, however, the key point is that both theories predict that a unipolar system will be peaceful.[57] Multipolarity is more dangerous to the world than unipolarity as past world wars were made possible and accelerated because of Great Powers rivalry.

For realists, knowledge of the structure of the international system stood out as the guiding light in what should shape prospects of things to come. John Mearsheimer was the first to gain attention in proclaiming an inevitable return to historical certainties when he stated that "the bipolar structure that has characterized Europe since the end of World War II is replaced by a multipolar structure" in which Germany, France, Britain, and perhaps Italy would assume major power status; the Soviet Union would decline from superpower status but would remain a major European power, giving rise to a system of five major powers and a number of lesser powers . Mearsheimer's main concern was that this shift in the shape of world order would create a far greater degree of insecurity than had existed under the relatively stable relationship built between the two poles during the Cold War years. In this analysis, deterrence was more difficult under multipolar conditions and balancing – the automatic response of sovereign states in a self-help system defined by international anarchy and power inequalities – would face difficult coordination problems that could result in miscalculation, escalation and war.[58] Many international scholars projected that in post-American period, there is going to be a multipolar world. The reappearance of European Union, the resurgence of Russia and the emergence of China are signs of the fulfillment of predicted multipolarity. The momentum of Turkish dream of neo-ottomans and powerful resistance of Iran would add to the possibility of changing world order.

In more than 70 years since World War II ended, the US has spent around 28 years, engaged in large-scale combat, causing the deaths of over 90,000 US military personnel. This includes the Korean War, the Vietnam War, the Afghan War and the War in Iraq and there have been other deployments in smaller conflicts. Nearly three decades over a 76-year period is a staggering amount of time for any nation to be at war. With the exception of Operation Desert Storm,[59] the US has not won any of these wars. Korean War[60] ended in an armistice, with both sides at roughly the same point as when they began. Vietnam War[61] ended with the Vietnamese flag flying over Saigon. Afghanistan, Iraq and the related wars did not end in outright defeat, but they have not ended in victory. Given that the United States crushed both Japan and, with the help of the Allies, Germany in World War II and emerged with overwhelming military power, the increased tempo of US military operations since 1945, combined with consistently unsatisfactory outcomes is a drain on any power.[62]

The United States as superpower is challenged militarily by Russia and China and that they have been spending billions of dollars. USA has all the hi-tech weapons used in its military adventurism all over the globe. USA is the largest military spender in the world. In terms of power, it can circumnavigate the entire world and that it polices the world's oceans. The globe is the consumer of American products but it is seen as the world dictator. But like a man, USA is facing so many problems that ultimately contribute to its unfortunate demise.

Part Three

The Symptoms of the Sick Empire

"Let me say this as clearly as I can...The United States is not and never will be at war with Islam"
-- US President Barrack Obama

Chapter Seven

The Signs of the Imminent American Collapse

America's time as the undisputed hegemon of the world might be coming to an end. For better or worse, the United States has been the unipolar superpower presiding over a world system it has designed in 1945. Thanks to a range of interconnecting problems, a growing number of observers now reason out that the security environment of the early-21st century is becoming inhospitable to the kind of dominance that Americans were used to. Nothing is certain, and previous similar prophecies have turned out to be premature. Nevertheless, the decline of America's relative power and the end of unipolarity is now a sufficiently possible scenario as to warrant a serious debate about alternative grand strategies and an alternative role in the world.[63] Since the disastrous 2003 war in Iraq and the 2008 global financial crisis, Washington has been facing the end of unipolar moment. Trump and his predecessor, Barack Obama, are probably the most different American presidents one can imagine. But their analyses of America's position in the world had much more in common than most people recognize. Both of them understood that America's ambition to remain the world's only superpower was unsustainable and indefensible. Both acknowledged the centrality of geo-economics in the 21st century. And both recognized that they would need to work with political regimes that did not share America's values and norms.[64] Barack Obama and Donald Trump inherited a crisis-tattered American Empire. They could not repair the damage any longer.

In understanding the American power in relation to the notion of its declining trajectory, there are four alternatives in power Maximization. This is an important thing that analyst should consider. The first conceptual type is the capability-gap maximizer. To think this way is to equate a grinding down of American superiority in abilities, in and of itself, with a decline in power. In this lens, it makes no sense to speak of the United States managing to sustain its power advantage despite a shrinking marginal lead in economic and military capabilities. The COVID-19 pandemic exposed the reality of China taking over US economy. American standing in the world has been significantly affected by its foreign policies especially dealing with the war in the Muslim world. The second type is the dominance maximizer. To think this way is to understand US power as the ability to compel compliance from other countries in response to particular demands. Superiority in national capabilities is important to a strategist prioritizing dominance, since success often depends on having the resources required to issue credible threats. US dominance in the international arena is in its lowest stage. The third type is the influence maximizer. This way of thinking shares with the dominance maximizer, a concern with relational outcomes, that is, the ability to deliberately steer the behavior of others. But it discounts the value of overt displays of coerced obedience. For a strategist prioritizing influence, US power should be measured by how frequently and closely the outcomes of international interactions correlate with those for which the US has advocated, especially in collective decision-making settings. The fourth and final conceptual type is the liberal order longevity maximizer. To think in this way is to identify American power with the established norms that constitute and underwrite the liberal rules-based world order.[65] Looking at these abovementioned four alternatives in power maximization, America could no longer sustain its position in the world as the sole superpower.

The destiny of US in global stage can be read by taking a look at what happened to the British Empire particularly on its war against Boers.[66] The war between Boers and British Empire marked the end of British imperial rule according to many historians. British forces used their new weapons to defeat the Boers but things went badly for Britain from the beginning. It had more men and better weapons and was fielding its best generals. But the Boers were fervent in defending themselves, knew the terrain, and adopted effective guerrilla tactics that relied on stealth and speed. The British Empire had suffered 45,000 casualties; spent half a billion pounds, stretched its army to the breaking point, and discovered enormous incompetence and corruption in its war effort. Its brutal wartime tactics, moreover, gave it a black eye in the view of the rest of the world. At home, all of this created, or exposed, deep divisions over Britain's global role. Abroad, every other great power opposed London's actions. They were friendless and isolated with the rest of its allies.[67] In comparison as Zakari pointed out another superpower, militarily unbeatable and indomitable, wins an easy victory from the beginning in Afghanistan and then takes on what it is sure will be another simple battle. The result is a quick initial military victory followed by a long, arduous struggle, filled with political and military blunders and met with intense international opposition. The analogy is obvious; the United States is Britain, the Afghanistan war is the Boer War and by extension, the United States' future looks depressing. And indeed, regardless of the outcome in Afghanistan, the costs have been massive. The United States has been overextended and distracted, its army stressed, its image sullied. So-called rogue states such as Iran and Venezuela and great powers such as China and Russia are taking advantage of Washington's inattention and bad fortunes. The familiar theme of imperial decline is playing itself out one more time. History is happening again.[68] The eyes of the world are focused on the defeat of US against the militarily weak Taliban. The unsophisticated military movement is surprisingly defeated the superpower of the time.

In his 1987 book, "The Rise and Fall of the Great Powers," British historian Paul Kennedy argued that for the most powerful nations, whose interests span the globe, the costs of their military commitments outweigh the benefits of empire. Eventually, imperial overstretch saps economic growth as resources are diverted to the costs of empire, and the dominant power's economy declines until it is no longer able to afford the military needed to sustain its position. That, in Kennedy's view, was the cause of each previous great power's decline and, he predicted, so it would be for the United States.[69] Trillions of dollars have been spent in America's war especially against the Islamic world. These US military exploits destroy the image and values of America as a torch-bearer of democracy and the rule of law. Guantanamo Bay and Abu Ghraib painted an irremovable mark in American history.

Another bad omen is the COVID-19 pandemic. The world was surprised by the coming of coronavirus and that truly it affected the global economy. The other effect of the COVID-19 crisis has been to shed light on some of America's existing weaknesses. In contrast to the actual impacts of COVID-19 on American power, these weaknesses have the potential to be far more consequential over the long-term. From political polarization to an increasingly illiberal foreign policy bent, America has a number of liabilities on its balance sheet. And while America also has a number of sources of strength, if these weaknesses are not addressed, they may ultimately result in relative decline, causing the US economy to fall behind China and other fast-growing economies.[70]

Moreover, in the last two decades, the UN and the so-called international law have been undermined left, right and center. The neocons' policies of bypassing the UN for Iraq war in 2003 proved to be one of the nails in its coffin but the final nails were hammered by the awareness within the Muslims, the response that Mujahideen gave to the US invasions and the penetration of Islam's political aspect within the Ummah. These aspects made it difficult for the US to exercise its will through the existing international law, which it had defined for its own benefit to begin with. Had it not been the resolve of the Iraqi Muslims in not accepting US occupation, the bypassing of the UN to invade Iraq might have been ignored but instead it became a pain in the neck. As if the humiliation of Iraq was not enough, the Brave Muslims of Syria took a stand that unfurled the mask of western imperialism completely and made the UN completely ineffective.[71] Analysts emphasized that the global conflict today is polarized by the power struggle between Zionist-liberal capitalism and the axis of resistance. Primarily, the axis of resistance is led by Iran against the international Zionism, which is obviously headed by Euro-US-Israeli alliances. In general, China, Russia, Iran, and Venezuela belong to resisting forces.

Erdogèn's New Ottoman Dreams

Revival means an improvement of the condition or strength of something. It is natural approach of any group of people, which wants to reclaim its lost glory. For instance, European Union was established to unite the entire continent to regain and revive the glory of (western) Rome. Russia today is nostalgic of Byzantine Empire and that Pres. Putin wants to reestablish the Third Rome.[72] The Zionist state of Israel plans for the rebuilding of the Third Temple.[73] In the same manner, Adalet ve Kalkinma Partisi (AKP) government of Turkey has burned the candle at both ends in pursuit of neo-ottomans.

Historically, Turkey's independence was officially recognized with the implementation of the Lausanne Treaty signed on 24 July 1923. This was after the defeat of the Ottoman Empire and its allies. The largest and powerful empire which stood for centuries was reduced to a single country and became secular for that matter. Britain and its allies then pulled out all their troops that had occupied Turkey since the end of the First World War. In response to this, protests were made in the House of Commons to the British Foreign Secretary Lord Curzon, for recognizing Turkey's independence. Lord Curzon replied and assured with confidence, "The situation now is that Turkey is dead and will never rise again, because we have destroyed its moral strength, the Caliphate and Islam." In 1924, the ottoman caliphate was abolished and would impossible to revive. This was guaranteed by British Empire and the allied forces. The reason why they exerted their utmost efforts to bring down and cripple Ottomans is Islam. Political Islam was and will always be a pronounced threat to the western world.

Evidently, all traces of Islamic political structures and institutions were lost as European powers decided the future of the whole planet. The present-day Arab world is heavily indebted of its political structures and institutions to the old European colonial powers that colonized it. However, after 1945, America emerged as the world's ruling state and entered the Arab world with the intention of displacing British and French influence, and usurping the oil fields of the Middle East. US President George Bush once said, "They (referring to Muslims) hope to establish a violent political utopia across the Middle East, which they call a "Caliphate" where all would be ruled according to their hateful ideology. I'm not going to allow this to happen – and no future American President can allow it either." As noted above, any Islamic political revival will be countered with power and strength. United States and the western world in general do not allow any emerging new order that directly comes in opposition to the west liberal order. AKP party led by President Erdogèn runs in harmony with the political Islam, which the Muslim Brotherhood put forward. Pres. Erdogèn[74] has been struggling to realize neo-Ottomanism employing many strategies and tactics: from "zero conflict with neighboring countries" to "conflict with all its neighbors." Turkey was one of the pillars and at the forefront of Arab Spring Project. Arab Spring was instigated to bring down western puppets that, in one way or the other, perpetrated and perpetuated corruptions that further embittered that miserable condition of the people. Muslim Brotherhood stood against the corrupt regimes in the Arab world. Many countries welcomed this uprising including Iran. Iranian government threw its support to the emerging revolution. This brought insecurities to the western-sponsored governments and thus plotted way out to stymie it. Al Jazeera covered the uprising 24/7 and Qatar supported the revolution.

The revolution, however, was powerfully responded with counterrevolution headed by western powers so that it would die a natural death. Dr. Muhammad Morsi, the leader of Muslim Brotherhood, was imprisoned along with several MB key leaders. Turkey received defeat with open hands. But it was not the end of the game. Part of the expansionist predilection, Turkey supported opposition in Syria to remove Pres. Assad. It started by lambasting President Assad over his state policies. It has also bolstered its influence in regional allies namely, Qatar, Sudan and Libya. As main alternative to US-led west, Turkey contracted a trade of S-400 with Russia.

Feffer addressed the fact that as a quintessential rising middle power, Turkey no longer hesitates to put itself in the middle of major controversies. He added that Turkish mediation efforts nearly heralded a breakthrough in the Iran nuclear crisis, and Ankara supported the flotilla that tried to break Israel's blockade of Gaza. With these and other less high-profile interventions, Turkey has stepped out of the shadows and now threatens to settle into the prominent place on the world stage once held by its predecessor.[75] Turkey, under the mighty hand of Erdogèn, has clearly dipped its hands in so many global issues and controversies. It was Turkey which buttressed Qatar during the Saudi-led blockade warning the Saudi-coalition of impending war if Qatar is attacked; Erdogèn deployed Turkish military in defense of Qatar. Turkey had also occupied Suaken Island in Sudan after its diplomatic overture to Sudanese leadership. Erdogèn has been so vocal against Israel. Gaza becomes Turkey's political capital in claiming the backing and sympathy of the Ummah. During Rohingya crisis, Turkey had also shown its support and assistance. In addition, President Assad once sarcastically said that Erdogèn is a self-styled "Caliph." He has been hurling destructive criticism on Syria, which is outside of his country.

The most visible reason why Turkey has been working in global stage is its so-called strategic revival of Ottoman Empire. In the seventeenth century, the Ottoman Empire was a force to be reckoned with, spreading through the Balkans to the gates of

Vienna before devolving over the next 200 years into the sick man of Europe. Conceivably, Feffer noted that Turkey occupies a vital crossroads between and among Europe, the Middle East and Central Asia. A predominantly Muslim democracy atop the ruins of Byzantium, it bridges the Islamic and Judeo-Christian traditions, even as it sits perched at the nexus of energy politics. All roads once led to Rome; today all pipelines seem to lead to Turkey. If superpower status followed the rules of real estate, then Turkey would already be near the top of the heap.[76]

Turkey is situated between and among the colliding major powers. AKP-led Turkey asserted its prominence in global politics. It is ready to look eye-to-eye with United States. In fact, it frustrated American plans in Mideast. During US-backed Gen. Haftar's military onslaught in Tripoli, Turkey was on the opposing side. It also purchased weapons from Russia, which is a mortal sin committed by any US ally that possibly causes to its fall. Though, there is a central miscalculation of the AKP and its intentions. Islamism has about as much influence in modern-day Turkey as communism does in China. In both cases, what matters most is not ideology, but the political power of the ruling parties. AKP has been steering Turkey away from its traditional route into a new road of Political Islam. Political Islam, as far as AKP ideology is concerned, means struggling within the secular system by enforcing Islam, though it is fenced by secular constitution. China, in its own right, is governed by one-party-system. Economic growth, political stability, and soft-power diplomacy regularly trump ideological consistency. Turkey is becoming more pro-home rule and more self-assured, and flexibility, not fundamentalism, have been the hallmark of its new foreign policy. Given the obsession of AKP-led Turkish government to neo-Ottomanism, it goes without saying that Kurds will become, once and for all, the first casualty.

Further than the abovementioned dreams of Turkey is its obsession with Hagia Sophia. Constantiniyya or Constantinople was the center of Christian world known as Rum in the Quran and that is prior to the schism. Western Latin-speaking Christians in what is now Rome in Italy, the center of Catholicism, separated from Eastern Orthodox Christianity. Hagia Sophia is formerly a cathedral, which was built by Emperor Justinian. When the construction was done, the Emperor, to his excitement, exclaimed, "I surpassed King Solomon." Why is it that it is and has always been surrounded by controversy since the beginning? The reason is that it is a Christian cathedral, which was converted into a Masjid when Ottomans overtook it. Conversion of the cathedral into a place of worship for Muslims was unprecedented in Islamic history. Caliph Omar did not do it with the churches in Palestine when he subjugated it. Salahudin did not also do the same. Hagia Sophia means Holy Wisdom. It is the second persona of the Christian Holy Trinity: Logo. It is an emblem of Jesus Christ. In postwar period when Atatùrk rose to power, he established a secular government patterned after Westphalian system, and then converted the Mosque into a museum. For the last time and as a part of Erdogèn's internal struggle within the secular system to realize reform and transformation, gradually, he is transforming Turkey into Islamic government. That means he is trying to form and institutionalize a political Islam in an evolutionary manner. He reconverted Hagia Sophia into a Masjid once again. The leadership of the whole Orthodox Christians around the world has condemned this act. There are two important things at play. Firstly, Erdogèn is fulfilling the end-time prophecy of the conquest of Constantiniyya using *takbir* and *tasbih* – devoid of war. If people may take a look at this, Turkey was the bastion of secularism in the Muslim world when Erdogèn came to power. Secondly, Erdogèn is testing its influence and power in the face of the western world.

On the issue of the betrayed Kurds, Right to Self-Determination is enshrined in the United Nations Charter and in numerous international laws and conventions. It is a known fact to all countries; therefore, the whole world must understand the situation of the Kurds. During the decolonization era, RSD became closely identified as people's anti-colonial rights. In post-war setting especially WWII, Entessar disclosed that a multilateral protection of human rights and ethnic rights received important attention to challenge the state-centric concentration of international law. Universal Declaration of Human Rights, which has been accepted as the main pillar of the international bill of rights, is considered as international customary law.[77]

Unfortunately, powerful countries that are supposed to take side on the betrayed and oppressed nations become silent sensing the undesirable effects of their actions. The problem lies on excessive nationalism that people are jailed by nation-state norm and that humanitarian political ethics deemed inoperable, unserviceable and impractical. Analysts can see the limitations of international legal remedies in augmenting minority rights in an international order controlled by state-centric views and institutions. Kurds had fought under the banner of allies during World War I. They fought bravely because they wanted free and independent nation, as promised to them, should the victory side with the allies. History, fortunately, sided with the allied forces. Britain based on the treaty of Sevres had to give Kurds an independent nation but after three years, Lausanne Treaty without due regard of the former treaty effectively abrogated it. The Republic of Turkey was announced that changed the borders. This is the first betrayal against the Kurds in modern times.

The second betrayal happened during the withdrawal of US from Syria. United States supported the Kurds in fighting the ISIS. The Syrian Democratic Forces (SDF), a coalition of Kurdish and Arabs, defeated ISIS and liberated eastern Syria. SDF lost eleven thousand forces, leaders and fighters who were engaging military combat with ISIS. The region controlled by Kurdish People's Protection Units – or popularly known as Yekineyen Parastina Gel (YPG) – the repeatedly targeted group is under attack as Turkey launches an operation dubbed Oplan Peace-Spring. The attack was primarily launched in order to create a safe zone and peace corridor.

Historically, for over four centuries in post-Arab conquest, the Kurds played an essential political role in western Asia. For instance, they provided important leaders in the Islamic world; the most notable of them was Salahudin-Al-Ayyubi who led the Muslims fighting against the crusaders. Entessar in his book titled, "Kurdish Ethnonationalism," related that the Kurds were not involved in major exploits beginning the fall of Abbasid Empire until the rise of Safavid Empire. The advent of Safavid dynasty and the ensuing rivalry between the Persians and the Ottoman Turks brought the Kurds to the fore as key players in Mideast politics. Both the Safavid dynasty and Ottomans view Kurdish-inhabited regions as buffer zones between their rival empires. In other words, the Kurds became a significant pawn in the Persian-Ottoman rivalry beginning in the early 16th century with the coming to power of Safavid Dynasty. Taking advantage of their Sunni fellow feeling, the Ottoman Sultans sought to attract the allegiance of the Kurds against the Shia Safavid. With the assistance of Sultan Salem of Ottoman dynasty, a number of Kurdish tribal leaders revolted against Safavid Dynasty. They were assets to ruling empires.

In 1639, an Ottoman-Safavid treaty was signed by Sultan Murad and Shah Abbas effectively designating the Kurdish region to the Ottoman Empire and Safavid Empire. Then division became the rule of the day. Kurds were either serving Ottomans or Persians. In the aftermath of World War I, while in the process of forging a new entity in Iraq, the British sought to assimilate the Kurds into the new Iraqi society by convincing the Iraqi Arabs to reserve some senior positions in the government for the Kurds. Yet, the Arabs opposed this scheme as they did not trust the Kurds. For the Arabs, while disregarding the fundamental principle of Islamic brotherhood have been treating the Kurds as others. In

1978, left-wing Kurds under the direction of Ocalan founded the Marxist Partiya Karkêr Kurdistanê (PKK), an organization whose goal was autonomy for Turkey's Kurds. The government beat the PKK to the brink of annihilation during the early 1980s. But Ocalan fled to Syria, where in 1984 he and his supporters regrouped and declared war on the Turkish government. The PKK launched a violent campaign aimed at weakening the government, following the examples of Peru's Shining Path and Cambodia's Khmer Rouge. PKK rebels allegedly have slaughtered thousands of Kurdish villagers who refused to support their cause, especially school teachers, whom they blamed for spreading Turkish propaganda.

Presently, Kurds are scattered and divided into several nationalities. There are Iraqi, Iranian, Syrian, and Turkish Kurds. They are extremely and highly divided as they have different political statuses in their respective countries. In Iraq, they have enjoyed autonomous status. They governed the Kurdistan Autonomous Government (KAG). Kurds especially the members of the Marxist-inspired PKK in Turkey are considered terrorists in the eyes of Turkish government. In Syria, they have occupied its northern part. It is a de facto autonomous region of Syria which is the epicenter of today's political earthquake in Mideast as far as US-Turkey relationship is concerned. The case of Iranian Kurds is different. They are not politically assertive and that they are virtually living in utter silence.

Still, the tension between US and Turkey is originated from US position in relation to Kurdish status. US wanted an empowered Kurds in order to counter ISIS and create a military balance in

Mideast effectively. Turkey does not want a stronger Kurds because it would lead to an empowered PKK. In retrospect, Turkey and Syria had once irreconcilable differences. Erdogen wanted Assad out. In fact, Turkey was accused of allegedly supporting ISIS just to facilitate the removal of Assad from the position of power but it was verified to be wrong later. The truth is that it supported secular Free Syrian Army (FSA) together with US but then it shifted to Muslim Brotherhood-inspired groups with the sole aim of changing the existing regional order. When Syrian Kurds led by SDF became so assertive and aggressive due to US backing, Syria and Turkey got closer. They had shared interests. Erdogèn did not want a rising Syrian Kurds because he was afraid and worried that an empowered Syrian Kurds might help the Turkish Kurds – namely PKK, which was seen as terrorist organization – staged powerful rebellion to Turkey. Assad, in his part, did not want an empowered Syrian Kurds because they might be used in regime-change plot of the Superpower.

Turkey-US alliance has been especially at conflicting situation. In the past, Turkey was at the beck and call of US. Though US-led NATO had been suffering internal conflict, Turkey is still a member. The most vital point is that US could no longer manipulate and control its allies abroad particularly the rising power such as Turkey.

The Conflict of States: The Case of United States of America and Islamic Republic of Iran

From the spectrum of international politics, Morgenthau opined that there are several elements of national power such as but not limited to the following, to wit: Geography, Natural Resources, Industrial Capacity, Military Preparedness and Population.[78] The most stable factor upon which the power of a nation depends is obviously geography. For instance, the fact that continental territory of United States is separated from other continents by bodies of water 3,000 miles wide to the east and more than 6,000 miles wide to the west is a permanent factor that determines the position of the US in the world. In other words, the geographical location of the US remains a fundamental factor of permanent importance that the foreign policies of all nations must take into account. However, its bearing upon political decisions might be today different from what it was in other periods of history. Second important element is natural resources including food, raw materials and oil. Natural resources are another relatively stable factor that exerts an important influence upon the power of a nation with respect to other nations. In times of war, country which has no enough food will most likely be defeated. Presently, the power of oil cannot be ignored. It is a fatal weapon of the producing countries against the consuming countries. Industrial capacity is a salient element of national power. United States has drawn a good deal of its natural strength from the possession of vast amounts of raw materials such as uranium because it possesses industrial plants that can transform it into industrial products. With its industrial plants, US can build and maintain a military establishment commensurate with its foreign policy. In addition, what gives the factors of geography, natural resources and industrial capacity their actual importance for the power of a nation is military preparedness. The dependence of national power upon military preparedness is so evident to need much explanation. Military preparedness requires a military establishment capable of supporting the foreign policies pursued. Last in the enumeration of elements of national power is population. Population matters. Without large population, it is impossible to establish and keep going the industrial plant necessary for the successful conduct of modern war; to put into the field the large number of combat groups to fight on land, on the sea, and in the air; and of course to fill the cadres of the troops considerably more numerous than the combat troops that must supply the latter with food, means of transportation and communication, ammunitions and weapons.[79]

In the above enumerated elements of national power, in the case of US and Iran standing, both are potent and great. USA is of paramount position in global arena because of its national power. Iran also is strong, powerful and in control of vast territory inside and outside of its national territory. The present US-Iran mayhem – though there is no full-scale war in the present– should be defused because it would be potentially distressing, disturbing and devastating.

As a matter of fact, after World War II, Great powers and nations were on the threshold of achieving reconciliation and peace. They established United Nations to ensure that war would be forever put into oblivion and that all the people could enjoy peaceful world. Unfortunately, UN became an arena of competition. The two victors had set the wheels in motion. From the birth of United Nations, countries around the world did not experience true peace and that it seems to be an empty promise. After the collapse of the bipolar system and the eventual takeover of unipolar system, wars have always been inseparable in the literature of world history. The international institutions were not that powerful enough to effect peaceful world. It has been argued and claimed that institutions push states away from war and promote peace. Institution is a set of rules that stipulate the ways in which states should cooperate and compete with each other. They prescribe acceptable forms of state behavior and proscribe unacceptable kinds of behavior. These rules are negotiated by states, which are standards of behavior defined in terms of rights and obligations. Sadly, Institutions have been used as instrument of powerful states to forward their respective national interests, foreign policies and influence. Moreover, realist-oriented US model in foreign policy and international politics highlights state-centric view. In a footnote, the states are actors and superior players in the international relations. It looks at the sacred self-centeredness of the nation-states as principal units of international system. Here, one can notice the contradicting orientations of institutionalism and realism, which both drag the international system in a rather grim world prospects.

The conflict between United States and Islamic Republic of Iran in Middle East is situated in the environment where a less functional institution – such as the Organization of Islamic Cooperation (OIC) and United Nations – and the conflictual function of international system exist. Given the established international system and after the postwar reconstruction, there are four Muslim responses to the challenge of imperialism and colonialism according to John Esposito in his book, "The Islamic Threat: Myth or Reality". These are the following: rejection; withdrawal; secularism and westernization; and Islamic modernism.[80] These diverse and variegated responses can form an idea why the Islamic world is still divided.

The division in the Islamic world is unqualified and absolute. It exists because of Muslims' penchant for ethno-nationalism, preservation of their entrenched national interests and their deep-seated power-struggle. Social Darwinism has found its way to the Muslim world. The divide when it comes to theology and politics does not need more elucidation. Sectarianism and Takfirism are salient variables in the study of present imperialism and interventionism in the Islamic world. Importantly, states were born from the bosom of one Muslim world. Finally, the rejection of Iran of the international order will inevitably be responded with a heavy blow. The Islamic world has produced myriad of personalities, who stood against the domineering western powers but they faced inevitable end in various ways. Abdulnasser, Qaddafi and Sayyid Qutb among others were erstwhile stellar actors in Islamic world who resisted the west but they failed to sustain their respective call for change. Presently, Iran (and to some extent Turkey) is introducing reforms at odds with western paradigm. In the empire of realism where nation-state acts as the most important player, confrontation and collision are normal. Realist point of view highlights the inevitability of strife, legitimacy of using force and promotion of national interests and the consolidation of the supremacy of state. In this way, US-Iran clash of interest is true.

Turkey, Saudi and Iran as Three Actors
United States has navigated the sea of challenges as a superpower starting from the destruction of Berlin Wall when communism ceased as a threat to western liberalism. America effectively displaced other major powers in Africa and Asia not to mention Americas as they are its backyards. US exported liberal capitalism around the world and being the leader of the western world, it has to dictate Europe and all its allies. After the red threat came the green threat (Islam). Islam was isolated in the international arena because of US powerful and deceptive diplomacy. To existing New World Order, Turkey is not a threat but it wanted its share in the pie. When people look at the present Republic of Turkey, they can sense two things: The state and Erdoğen. The Republic of Turkey, on one hand, is a secular state. It has all the elements of secular government. On the other hand, there is an internal struggle of Pres. Erdoğen within the secular system. Erdoğen was the Prime Minister of Turkey for more than a decade. Those times, Prime Minister holds the reins of executive and legislative power. He was the head of government while the president was only a ceremonial head of state.

Last 2017, there was a constitutional amendment, which changed the system from titular president to a stronger president. Republic was, later on, at the behest of Erdogèn. He appeared the paramount power in Turkey. He became active, assertive and supportive to the Ummah. He had and has been criticizing Israel consistently. Erdogèn touched every international issue besetting the Muslim world from Rohingya crisis to Libyan political tug of war, from Qatar blockade to Moro nation-building and from Sudan's political fissures to refugee crisis. Surprisingly, at the peak of Syrian conflict, Turkey shot down Russian fighter plane. Internationally, Turkey is faced with multifarious crises challenging the new world system. Fortunately, Erdogèn sustains his internal war. Therefore, Turkey is not a threat to the empire but Erdogèn is. Turkey under the leadership of Erdogèn is unwavering to realize neo-Ottomans whether it is through cooperation with NATO or with the Ummah. In one occasion, he criticized Israel and the west but in other occasion he had to follow the diktats of US-led NATO.

In comparison, in 1979, a real threat appeared in Iran. The threat is not Imam Khomeini: it is his ideology. The rise of Imam Khomeini with his *Wilaya al-Faqih* became a political threat to democracy and capitalism. Iran since the very beginning has been in a state of resistance because the superpower does not want a system runs in opposition to liberal democracy. Scholars have correctly pointed out that threat to capitalism and democracy is not socialism of China and Russia. The ideological threat is in Iran. Therefore, the conflict today is between western liberal capitalism and the emerging Iranian Revolution. Iranian people destroyed secular western-backed Shah

System.[81] The main difference between Turkey and Iran is that the former puts forward its Islamic revolution to working within the confines of secular system while the latter performs its Islamic revolution by destroying the system itself. In addition, Turkey focuses on international level while Iran concentrates only in Middle East.

Many international thinkers and analysts have been putting forth that there would be a war between Iran and US in the future because of ideological differences. To note, after the death of communism,[82] liberal capitalism became the only international ideology. It was exported and sold in the global market. The whole world embraced it. China and Russia are powers and military counterweights to US. The socialism of China is not international ideology to be exported to other parts of the world. It is enough for China to be a regional player and it has to defend its territory. It would not export its brand of socialism until the Coronavirus arrived. In the post-pandemic period, China would change its course as it would police the world after America.

The current regional order in Middle East – specifically the Arab World – is created by the two colonial masters namely, France and Great Britain. France and Britain divided Middle East through Sykes-Picot Agreement in 1916, a century ago. This means that

Levant or Sham (Syria and Lebanon) is France's spoils of war while the larger part of Arabia would be given to Britain. The French empire had been so obsessed with Levant starting from the colonial era. France had penetrated Ottoman Empire through its agent Muhammad Ali Pasha, the man who almost toppled the caliph in Istanbul. He was a governor of Egypt who was from Balkan Peninsula; he was European in race. He was also once called the "the hammer of the Caliph" who brought Ibn Saud to his knees. Even during the Ottoman era, French Empire successfully convinced the Sultan of Istanbul to let Catholics of Levant live under France's guiding hands.

Colonial lords constructed this regional order with three pillars: Iran, Turkey and Saudi Arabia. Iran was entrusted to the Shah while Turkey was to Kemalist leaders. Britain pegged al-Saud to Saudi Arabia. This was how the Muslim countries and Mideast states in particular were controlled. During the dying moments of British Empire in Suez Canal, US abandoned it which gave birth to the shifting of the concentration of power. Then, America had taken over the possession of British Empire. In 1979, the Shah of Iran was toppled by the Iranians led by Imam Khomeini. The "Island of Stability" erupted. It was a great US tragedy ever. During the infancy of Iranian revolution, US had to put it to a complete halt. However, it was a useless attempt. In 2003 or so, Erdogèn rose to power in Turkey. His Islamist tendency shook Washington and Brussels. Turkey – under his leadership – did not divorce Europe and Washington but it established a say principally in regional level. It is still a member of NATO but not passive and silent. Turkey did not shoot a single bullet when Libya was invaded by NATO. Erdogèn has been so assertive when it comes to defending the welfare of Muslims around the world and in Mideast in specific. He is so noisy when it comes to Palestinian issue. He is ready to lambaste Israel without fear, though many analysts see it as political rhetoric. The two stakes in Mideast are crumbling and that only Saudi is still standing. The "deal of the century" or the so-called recognition of Jerusalem as Israel's capital is not isolated case in an overall Mideast trouble. Analysis suggests that one of the reasons of this deal of the century is to give to Saudi the custodianship of Masjidil Aqsa in Jerusalem to boost its influence in the Muslim World. The current custodian of Masjidil Aqsa is Jordan. Another candidate for custodianship is Turkey.

The present aggressiveness of states and republics in Middle East is saber-rattling. What is even worrying is the emergence of nuclear states, which would change the landscape of traditional warfare. Nuclear war could destroy the planet rapidly and would perish us all. For instance, the first and ever nuclear attack had killed tens of thousands if not hundreds in a minute or less. Unquestionably, one philosophy puts forward the idea that possession of nuclear weapons could be a mechanism to prevent wars. This is the dominant and prevalent mindset. The question is that if history has an account of nuclear attack, how can we assure that there would be no attack in the future?

The rivalry of the Great Powers reached the war-torn and battle-scarred Yemen. Yemen is inseparable fragment of the whole Ummah. It is as ancient nation as Middle East civilization. It has a remarkable role in the tremendously changing Mideast. It is a home of great people. Yemen is appeared and depicted in international media as pitiful, abandoned and miserable country. Though, it is undergoing world's worst humanitarian crisis in the present, it has rich and distinct history. It pioneered unrivalled civilization. More than half a decade had passed since the invasion of Saudi-led coalition, still the problem remains unresolved and even getting more complicated and escalating. Sadly, civilians are the victims of aerial bombs, suicide bombings, movement restrictions, lack of basic services and humanitarian blockade. The maelstrom of foreign occupation and national crisis has no end in sight.

The present situation in Yemen is dismal and calamitous. The powerful countries in the world are silent in the face of Saudi-led invasion of a country with people virtually living in hunting age. Saudi Arabia has purchased sophisticated and state of the art weapons, missiles, military equipment and even air defense systems from the Major Powers. The powerful military industries in US, Britain and France have sold weapons to Saudi Arabia, which are being used to combat Houthis adversely affecting the civilian populations. Saudi purchased weapons costing hundred billion dollars. The United Arab Emirates (UAE) has been doing the same. These two countries are living in luxury. They have towering buildings and other infrastructures. They have glass towers. They are competing since the onset of development boomed by Oil Industry, which countries could build the tallest building on earth. These riches and wealth brought into existence because of oil. This wealth is not acquired by hardworking but of discovery, which should be distributed to the poor. Yemenis suffer unspeakable poverty and their lives are characterized by backwardness. The never-ending war in

Yemen is another symptom of the declining superpower. It can no longer police the world and it is incapable of influencing international situation.

On US hegemonic approach to conflict, it does not respect international law. There is an existential international law that all nations around the world must submit to even the self-proclaimed superpower. There is inherent and inviolable sovereign right that every single nation on earth must enjoy. The bedrock of United Nations is built upon the policy of respect and non-interference on the internal affairs of a country. In the bipolar era, the world is blindsided by the suspension of this policy when the two self-proclaimed superpowers had entered every nation. They forcibly divided the world. Every country was either satellite camp of Russia or US. There was no United Nations during that time. In the "purposes and principles" of United Nations charter, it states, "The purpose of UN is to develop friendly relations among nations based on respect for the principle of equal rights and self-determination of peoples and to take other measures to strengthen universal peace" (article 1). In Article 2, it states, "the organization is based on the principle of the sovereign equality of all its members." This exposition suggests that every single nation must respect others for the preservation of the universal peace.[83]

Based on the foregoing, the US military deployment in so many countries especially in Syria is a violation for the two following grounds: (1) US came without Syria's invitation; and (2) US mobilized and trained the rebels. These are the two main among several reasons why US violated the principle of UN. Based on the principle of UN, every member shall develop friendly relations with one another. As a token of respect, US should not deploy military to Syria because Syria is a UN member-state. In fact, the former should employ a courtesy to the country. US funded, mobilized and trained the rebels in Syria in order to bring down Assad's government. Big resources from American taxpayers will only go to the brutal rebels who violated, denigrated and attacked violently the peaceful Muslim and Christian communities in Syria.

The Rising China and the Islamic World

The Mao period lasted from 1949 to 1977, and witnessed the deaths of millions of people from hunger and the killing of millions of others. Strict discipline prevailed in all areas of life, little individual freedom was allowed and whole communities were kept in line by violence and oppression. Deng Period started from 1978 up to the present. In this period, China opened its border to international market and investment. The western companies and corporations were able to grab the opportunity to invest in China. While Mao and Deng have significant differences both in theory and practice, looking at them from a wider perspective, based on the criteria of rule of law, human rights and democracy, two very important similarities exist in the two periods. Throughout both periods the country was kept under the stringent and austere control of the Communist Party. The present leaders are also enduring to suppress the Chinese people especially the Uighurs and other minority groups under that same despotic regime.

Azizuddin El-Kaissouni, a graduate of the American University in Cairo, shared that it is of little surprise that China, like so many other countries, has chosen to take advantage of September 11 to further its own political agenda and silence the internal dissent. All recent human rights reports would point to a drastic escalation of persecution and repression against the Uighur minority.[84] UN High Commissioner Mary Robinson expressed her concern over the treatment of the Uighurs. The Chinese government, predictably, responded that "terrorism" that ephemeral and much-abused term is an infringement of human rights and is a threat to international peace and security. The Human Rights Watch report is also particularly illuminating. The report describes the various forms of repression and persecution suffered by the Muslims of Eastern Turkistan under Chinese rule. According to Amnesty's report, on Fridays, schools force Muslim students to stay in school for lunch in order to prevent them from going to prayer. Furthermore, Muslims under the age of 18 are not allowed to enter mosques or to receive any sort of religious education. Implemented nowhere else in China, the article 14 of the Xinjiang Uyghur Autonomous Region (XUAR) regulation entitled "Implementation Measures of the Law on the Protection of Minors" states that parents and legal guardians may not allow minors to participate in religious activities. The OIC insisted that Beijing must do more to bring justice to

---

Xinjiang. Tellingly, since the very beginning, OIC has been calling upon the Government of China to carry out prompt, effective and transparent investigation of these grave incidents and bring those responsible to quick justice and to take all possible measures to prevent its recurrence. Chinese government has been clearly violating the basic and fundamental rights of Uighurs. The right to choose religion and then practice its rituals is fundamental human right. No one has the power to deprive others of this basic right.

Communism is inherently anti-religious ideology. It says religion is opium of the society. It reduced religion as mere garbage. China is ruled by one state party—Communist Party of China (CPC). Xinjiang is one-sixth of the entire Chinese territory. Removing it will damage Chinese resources and revenues. With centralized structure, China has to put Xinjiang under its sphere of influence. This autonomous administration has to be controlled. Economically, Xinjiang is home to rich natural resources. Theoretically, all countries around the world would willingly fight just to defend resources. Wars happen because of economic competition and rivalry. China will not give the resources of Xinjiang even at the expense of persecuting its own people. Strategically, Xinjiang is sitting at the front of Afghanistan and Pakistan. That's why it is a good buffer zone.

The rise of China is phenomenal. USA has been heavily indebted to China. It has a debt of staggering more than 2 Trillion dollars to China. If China will request US to pay its debt in Euro, it could be so painful and catastrophic. China is a rising power cultivating the trenches of multipolar world. In this development, it has to employ win-win solution on Xinjiang Question. RSD can be expressed in independence and genuine autonomy arrangement. If China is hard-pressed in freeing East Turkistan, at least genuine autonomy is handed over, and in the long run, empowering autonomous region will also benefit the central government. The state of affairs in East Turkistan is reminiscent of a region persecuted under Maoism. The solution lies in giving what is due to the Uighurs. The oppression of Chinese government to its people cannot escape the sentinel of the US. As a sole superpower, theoretically, it has all the influence to stop and thwart this ill-treatment. The fact that US was and is still unable to stop China from oppression establishes a fundamental truth that it is incapable of bringing all countries to justice.

China throughout history has been an important player in global stage. There are four periods of Chinese history: Confucianism, Colonialism, Communism and Capitalism. Millennia have passed before the sunrise of western civilization, country now known as China was divided into dozens of viciously warring feudal states. From this disorder arose the most influential man in Chinese history: Confucius. Confucius introduced the notion of li – proper social behavior or respect of social order. His philosophical views were so dominate in Chinese history. The next period in the colonialism which is popularly known as "Century of Humiliation," the time when British Empire brought China to its knees. Communism was adopted by China as its ideology during bipolar moment. Under Mao's leadership, China adopted a Soviet-style planned economy with rigid government control. After the death of Mao in 1976, Deng Xiaoping became the paramount leader in China. He introduces capitalism in modern China's economy. He called it "Socialism with Chinese Characteristics."[85] The Chinese people have learned a lot from turbulent history of China. China takes over the position of US at the global level. The fact of the matter is that the Pentagon in September 2020 published its annual review of military and security developments involving China. The annual assessment, legally required by the Congress concluded: "China has already achieved parity with – or even exceeded – the United States in several military modernization areas, including shipbuilding, land-based conventional ballistic and cruise missiles and integrated air defense systems.[86]

Given the increase of China's power while Uighur Muslims are persecuted, oppressed and religiously restricted, still many Muslim countries have been allies and friends of China. The Ummah sees China as alternative partner in lieu of US. Iran and Pakistan, potential regional powers, are important friends of China. The only difference between US and China's treatment to Muslims is that the former would invade Muslim lands to perpetuate its insatiable interests while the latter is particular with its national security.

The Rise of Trump and America's Decline

President Donald J. Trump had sworn in January 2017 as 45th president of the United States of America. He signed a destiny-making executive order of banning seven Muslim-majority countries from entering US. This policy would, once and for all, precipitate the deep-rooted divide between the Judeo-Christian world and the Ummah. This bold decision would have tremendous religious upheaval especially Christianity and Islam in US and the world at large. Trump rhetoric might appear as Christian stance to the detriment of Muslim-Christian relations. Religious extremists appeared in America in droves. Americans viewed that Evangelical Christians in their eschatological narrative believed that Christianity's last bastion is America.

Historically, evangelicalism is a movement emerged from Protestantism. During catholic-protestant divide in Europe, Protestants migrated to the then US of America. They believe that America has a monumental role in the advent of Jesus Christ. They are longing for the second coming of Christ. In addition, it had been a principle and a culture in international relations and foreign policy-making, in any nation since the dawn of world political history, that diplomacy is of paramount consideration as peace overture even in times of conflict. The creation of UN signaled the age of diplomacy in favor of war and exclusivism between and among the family of nations. In cold war heyday, the politics of bipolar system dominated the international relations. It was this period when the two superpowers had divided the world into two groups: the 'politically quarantined nations' and 'politically free nations'. The quarantined are those weak nations, especially Muslim countries. The 'politically free nations' were the superpowers, which observe no bounds and laws.[87] They consider as essential or of vital interest and absolutely justified the launching of aggression, colonization, exploitations and enslaving nations. In the twilight of this bipolar system, emerged the unipolar system in which the world is governed by solo superpower, i.e. USA. President Trump occupied the pulpit of global leadership. He was the most powerful man on earth who bullied the figurehead secretary-general of United Nations. Not a week had passed when he became a president, he sent his ambassador to UN to bully it saying that UN must not come between US pro-Israeli stance or else there would be consequences.

After enjoying superpower status for decades, US had seen no significant obstacle to perpetuate its global supremacy except the rising sun of political Islam. In the first year of 21st century, Islam had appeared in the headlines of international media, which turned out as ghost to American global interests. Interestingly, US of America had that gargantuan wealth because of Middle East natural wealth e.g. oil, natural gas, etc.

Trump banned Muslims from entering US for several reasons: First, terrorism was the reason why Trump had to ban these seven countries. He would like to guard the American people from the scourge of terrorism from the so-called Muslim Terrorists. Ironically, war on terror was one of the most deceptive projects in the history of America. This war is a euphemism of war on Islam. It destroyed the relationship of world religions especially Islam against every religion in the world. Former President Bush when he bombastically voiced out before the UN member states, "Either you are with us or with the terrorists," every single country had bowed down and submitted to this high-sounding threat. The Buddhists in China and Myanmar, Hindus in India, Jews in Israel and Christians in different countries came to the rescue of US, which was shedding crocodile tears. They bombed Iraq, Afghanistan, Yemen, Syria, Pakistan and Libya. The Muslim world was in awe over this scripted war.

Second, Trump had to execute this immigration policy because he wanted to save America from its timely downfall. At least, he had to prolong its irreversible decline. Politically, US could no longer hold the neck of EU and other allies. Brexit project appeared to the international media. Probably, Brexit was a means of Great Britain to leave America's dictatorship. In fact, Great Britain thwarted US interest in Libya. Economically, USA was teetering on the edge of collapse. One important reason of this economic insolvency was its war around the world. War would facilitate the death of a nation because there was a need to fund a war. Trump probably wanted to avoid direct war and so-called terrorism right on American soil. So, he had to prevent the possible entry of large-scale so-called terrorist attacks in his country. The reputation and dignity of US in the global audience have been significantly affected because of its war on terror. Tortures in Guantanamo Bay and Abu Ghraib have been equated to American values. The liberal capitalist values have been shattered to the core. Many countries around the world have been walking in caravan to migrate from the fantasy-land of American capitalist values to the lands of destiny where they would find solution to all their woes.

President Trump took an America First approach to trade and international affairs. Trump defined American global interests in transactional terms and repeatedly called for allied countries, including Germany, Japan, Saudi Arabia, and South Korea, to compensate the US for helping protect their nations. President Trump repeatedly threatened to walk away from alliances that no longer seemed to be paying dividends, regardless of old friendships or cultural affinities.[88] Trump's main foreign policy positions were to work with Russia unlike with his predecessors who treated it as an archenemy. This is the reason why during Trump's presidency, there was no massive conflict between Russia and US. Trump spoke of the need to deal with China, which was allegedly manipulating its currency at the expense of US consumers. For Trump, dealing with China included reconsidering at tariffs, intellectual property and bringing jobs back to America. The trade war between the two countries was upsetting and shocking that has impact on global economic crisis.

American democracy during 2020 election was tested and the world was surprised because of the deep divide between the followers of Biden and Trump. The followers of Trump could not accept the victory of Biden to such an extent that they vandalized the Capitol Hill, which is the symbol of American civilization. America was on the brink of civil war especially in post-poll setting. This divide remains alive and will potentially be reignited in the future.

The Russia's Comeback

Soviet Russia faced a fundamental problem, which led to its demise in 1990. There was an irreparable damage to its very ideology. China, which was a communist country, left Russia and favored the alliance of the west. After the death of Mao, China reinvented itself, Deng Xiaoping succeeded him as leader in China. At the age of sixteen, he went to France as a working student. Among many young and idealistic student revolutionaries, he stood out as pragmatist. When he became the leader of China, he introduced capitalism in China's economy. He called it "Socialism with Chinese characteristics." China abandoned Russian ideology. Subsequent to Russia's fall, US-led western world colonized Russia thereby facing westernization. Russia followed the model of west in terms of system and leadership.

The catastrophic collapse of the Soviet Union in 1991, and the West's total and unconditional backing for Yeltsin and his oligarchs changed the situation. Instead of trying to help Russia, the USA and the West used every single opportunity to weaken Russia externally. Internally, the West supported the Jewish oligarchs who were literally sucking out wealth of Russia while supporting every imaginable form of separatism.[89]

The US became the only superpower without one challenging its superiority over the rest of the world until the rise of Vladimir Putin in Russia. He recreated Russia from a mere colony to a powerful country. Russia came back to the scene of world politics. He had a mission to remove Russia from the orbit of Atlantic Integrationists. He reorganized the former Soviet Republics and was able to kick out US from Central Asia. During Putin's years, Collective Security Treaty Organization (CSTO), a military organization that served as counterweight of NATO, was organized. Also, Shanghai Cooperation Organization (SCO) was established as a political security organization with Russia and China as its two leader countries. China, Kazakhstan, Kyrgyzstan, Russia, Tajikistan and Uzbekistan are the current members. Possible candidates for membership are Afghanistan, India, Iran, Mongolia and Pakistan while Belarus, Sri Lanka and Turkey are dialog partners. The near-future SCO would thus include all of the following full members: such as China, India, Iran, Kazakhstan, Kyrgyzstan, Pakistan, Russia, Tajikistan and Uzbekistan.

Putin was able to create a name in Russia that will be remembered forever. His popularity is beyond question. He is one of the Great Leaders who have ever appeared in all history. Politically, he has been leading Russia for two decades now. The Russian constitution was amended that would authorize him to lead until 2036. He took Eurasian territories away from US influence. Eurasian borders remain as strategic areas of US-Russia competition. Economically, one of the priorities of Putin administration is his Arctic ambition. Definitely, energy has for long played a key role in bankrolling Russia's global ambitions throughout the last century. The high oil prices in the last decade played a central role in creating the narrative for Putin, who successfully navigated the country out of the post-Soviet decade of tragedy. The primary market of Russia's Liquefied Natural Gas (LNG) is India while Arctic Oil is China. Militarily, Russia is still a nuclear power. It has more nuclear warheads than US. During Putin's period, Russia has accelerated its hypersonic weapons. To meet the requirements as "hypersonic," an object would have to move at least five times the speed of sound and that it would be able to evade counter-fire and strike with great precision. Like US, Russia has its own private military company known as The Wagner Group. It has expanded its reach significantly especially in Africa. It trains the military in Sudan and Libya. It has participated in military parades in the Central African Republic (CAR). The UN estimates that more than 1,000 Wagner members are fighting alongside Khalifa Haftar (Libya). *When Putin announced plans to partially withdraw from Syria, he in reality offset this with private military companies. The advantage of using private military company is that if the soldiers would violate human rights, Russia will not be directly held accountable.*

Jerusalem in a Declining America

At the outset, when God talked to Abraham promising a piece of land in what is now Israel and Palestine, the tone of the promise is genetic and biological. It is a promise to his Semitic children—not to the white-skinned, blue-eyed and blonde. The state of Israel is densely-populated by almost 90 percent of the converted Jews from European descent. During the Abbasid Empire, when Muslims marched towards Europe to conquer, they met a king in Southern Russia, who belonged to Turkic people. His kingdom is known as Khazarian Empire.

One day, he gathered a multitude and called religious scholars from Christians and Muslims. In a meeting, he asked first the Muslim scholar, "What can you say about Christianity and Judaism?" And the Muslim scholar replied, 'we shared beliefs only that we do not believe Jesus being worshipped by Christians as God'. Then the Christian scholar was asked, 'what can you say about Islam and Judaism?' The scholar replied: 'we shared beliefs only that we do not believe Muhammad as prophet of God.' What can you say about Moses? The two replied: he is a noble prophet of God. After the debate, the King announced to the public and wanted all his subjects and the ruled in the Khazarian Empire to embrace Judaism because only Moses had that pure and impeccable personality and value that no one came and criticized him. There started the white-skinned Jews. An exchange letters from the Jewish Doctor of Spain and the King of Khazars had fascinatingly described the whole story.

There was a Jew working in Cordoba, Islamic Spain, named Hasdai Ibn Shaprut. He was born into a wealthy family and trained not just in Hebrew but in Latin and Greek. As legend has it, he got the attention of the Caliph because of his studies on poisons and their antidotes. As the highest-ranking Jew in the court of the Caliph, he was treated as leader of the Jewish community.[90] Jews of Spain were in the habit of making contact with Jewish communities throughout the world. So, it was natural for Hasdai to write a letter to Joseph, the King of the Khazars, when he learned of the conversion. The content of the letter is as follows:

> "I, Hasdai, son of Isaac, son of Ezra, belong to the exiled Jews of Jerusalem in Spain, the servant of my lord, the King, bow to the earth before him and prostrate myself towards the abode of your majesty from a distant land. I rejoice in your tranquility and magnificence and stretch forth my hands to God in heaven that he may prolong your reign in Israel."

It was several years before Hasdai received a response from Joseph explaining the complicated history that had led to the conversion of his people. According to Joseph in his letter to Hasdai,

The King searched, inquired, and investigated carefully and brought the sages together that they might argue about their respective religions. Each of them refuted, however, the arguments of his opponent so that they could not agree. When the King saw this, he said to them: Go home, but return to me on the third day. On the third day he called all the sages together and said to them, "Speak and argue with one another and make clear to me which is the best religion."

They began to dispute with one another without arriving at any results until the King said to the Christian Priest, "What do you think of the religion of the Jews and the Muslims, which is to be preferred?" The priest answered: "The religion of the Israelites is better than that of the Muslims." The King then asked the Qadi (Muslim Scholar and Judge): "What do you say? Is the religion of Israelites or that of the Christians, preferable?" The Qadi answered: "The religion of the Israelites is preferable." Upon this the King said: "If this is so, you both have admitted with your own mouths that the religion of Israelites is better. Wherefore, trusting in the mercies of God and the Power of the Almighty, I choose the religion of Israel, that is, the religion of Abraham. If that God whom I trust, and in the shadow of whose wings I find refuge, will aid me, He can give me without labor the money, the old and the silver which you have promised me. As for you all, go now in peace to your land."[91]

Judaism penetrated Europe from there, in addition to the wandering Jews in Europe. The Jews, who were forcedly driven away from their ancestral lands, found new parklands where they could enjoy and practice their religion. From there, the genius of the Jews penetrated the hall of European politics, economy and culture. They were able to influence leaders in Europe, specifically British Empire, which culminated in the openhandedly giving of the land of Israel in 1917—this is known in history as Balfour Declaration. It is the British Crown that planted the seed of Israel in Middle East and then watered by America daily. It is now growing that the neighboring Muslim countries have been overshadowed by its leaves, but they are unable to see the light of the sun of Ummah. Making Jerusalem as a capital of Israel is thought-out, if not the grand plan, of the deracinated Jews started when they were evacuated from their homes in 70 AD. The destruction of Jerusalem was complete. They roamed around the world and every Yom Kiffur celebration, they say, "Next year will be in Jerusalem." In their houses, wherever they are, there hanging text in the door, "Next year is in Jerusalem." In other words, it is a prearranged long in the tooth.

International recognition of Zionism was an important feature for the flourishing ideology. If Zionists could present their case to the world's leading powers and recruit their support, it would stabilize the foundations required against its critics to the eventuality of a national Jewish home. This recognition was initially founded by way of the Balfour Declaration. It demonstrated itself in its entirety in the establishment of the State of Israel thirty years later. British policy would enormously influence the shaping of the Middle East and the futures of both Arab and Jew.[92] Arab opposition was much swifter. Even though the Arabs would be granted eight percent of the land, the most fertile land had been allocated to the Jewish state. Furthermore 250,000 Arabs living in the Galilee would have to be transferred when they constituted ninety percent of the population.[93] Palestine was colonized by British Empire and later awarded to the Zionist movement. Since 1948, Palestine has been undergoing oppression perpetuated by the Zionist state while the Muslim world is virtually silent. Muslim leaders are good in rhetoric without defending the Palestinians both militarily and diplomatically except for an endless condemnation. Palestine has been immensely politicized, fundamentally used for dominance and leverage, and profoundly manipulated by self-proclaimed heroes of Muslims to get the attention of Ummah for enormous, engraved and eternal interests. World leaders in the past and at present have been at the forefront of using Palestine to create a self-made statue of bravery and gallantry. Palestine has been suffering numerous unspeakable mayhems and bedlams brought about by negligence of world leaders mainly the Muslim world. There are numberless pronouncements of condemnation from Muslim leaders once in a while but would only fall to deaf ears and that Zionist State continues to grab the lands of the Palestinians. The fact of the matter is that such condemnation is devoid of power and influence because of their

---

dependence to the western world. "Jerusalem is the red-line" has been the recycled rhetoric by many Arab leaders but since the founding of the Zionist State, the de facto and de jure capital of Israel is Jerusalem. The Knesset, which is the seat of power of Israel, is in Jerusalem. President Erdogen is seen by many as the hero of Islam but the truth is that he stands on America's back to realize his neo-Ottomanism. His one foot is on NATO while the other is on Ummah. He has been in power for almost two decades but he did not care and bother to think for a day to cut Turkey's diplomatic relations with the Zionist State. The reality is opposite: Turkey is a home to a training camp of Zionist forces and home to nuclear missiles of US. When time comes that US-Russia nuclear war breaks out, it would be through Turkey where Russia is hit back. So, whatever he says about defending Palestine is only a political rhetoric devoid of substance. Turkey under his administration is quick on responding war-torn countries such as Libya, Syria, Armenia, Iraq and many other Muslim countries. Why not in Palestine?

Moreover, NATO is the armed wing of the western world, which unfortunately Turkey is inseparable with – i.e. NATO and Turkey have been at best joined at the hip. The Zionist State is the outpost of NATO in Middle East. Turkey dances while US beats the drum. It is not by accident that as the old order created by colonial powers is on the deteriorating trajectory, the Zionist state has to grab that opportunity to rise. The post-American world is characterized by the transfer of power from west to the rest. While this unfolding drama in the holy land is perceived as typical conflict, it is an extra ordinary step toward getting long-term plan done. This is the right moment for the Zionist State to realize its long dream of taking the Al-Aqsa. What is happening at present might become worse in the future. While US is in power, the Zionist state would have to grab the chance to get its plan happened.

But how could Israel rule the Arabs and eventually the world with its peanut-sized territory? The Zionist State could govern the world the way British Empire, French Empire, Portuguese Empire, Spanish Empire and The Netherlands did in colonial times. British Empire ruled the world by its 48,000 forces with 17,000 reserved and left in its territory in defense of Catholic foes. The lands where Israel stands – not to mention the great frontier of promised land – is the most strategic area of the world sitting in the large freshwater reserves, which is the next gold and among the most precious elements on earth . Unfortunately, when the Islamic world chooses to leave Palestine in the hands of fate and let the oppression exist, then Israel will unquestionably become the ruling state. It can be prevented by the will of God should there be solidarity and unity among the Ummah.

With the help of the League of Nations[94] and then United Nations Israel remained stronger after more than 70 years. It fought major wars against its Arab neighbors. The lands and territory of Israel are becoming bigger and that the West Bank and Gaza are at the mercy of Israel. Hundreds of houses were constructed in West Bank by Israeli settlers in the midst of bulldozing homes of the Palestinians. Middle East is in a deep crisis. Iranians, Arabs and Turks are busy in power struggles. Iranian nation exported its revolution to Mideast while Saudi countered this growing influence of Iran. Turkey is asserting its expansionist ambition. These three inheritors of Islamic Empire are in conflict with one another. Each one wants to influence the current regional order. Their competition appeared so clear in Syria.

This regional conflict is especially a hotbed of Israel's future approach to Middle East. The Arabs are now in the sphere of Israel's influence. United Arab Emirates and Israel have signed agreements aiming to normalize situation in Middle East. UAE is a tiny and yet powerful force in the region. It backed Southern Front in Yemen, which frustrated Iran and Saudi's interests. It supported Eritrea when it was almost on the verge of war with Ethiopia. It supplied General Haftar with powerful weapons in Libya and thwarted the policies of Qatar, Turkey and Tunisia. Additionally, Turkey's forces had so many military encounters with Hezbollah in Syria. The military prowess of these three countries was utilized against one another while Israel is happily maneuvering and directing the situation. The scene unveils a perfect timing for Israel to launch a big war to reclaim the so-called biblical Holy Land. What happened in Lebanon is an indispensable piece of analysis. Hezbollah sits and influences Lebanon. Myriad of problems emerged such as financial crisis, social unrest and the powerful blast. The immediate effect of the blast was the mass resignation in the Lebanese parliament. All of this has effect in the weakening of the resistance to Israel. When Lebanon falls, Israel will be able to advance its regional policies. When Israel invades and takes the Promised Land, then it would become the powerful state in the world. Promised Land is more or less the present Israel, Palestine, Jordan, some parts of Syria and Iraq. These lands are rich in natural resources and freshwater. Promised Land is a strategic place sitting between the three continents. Moreover, Jordan is a place of great significance in the past and in the future as well. It has the Jordan River which possesses freshwaters. Freshwater will become more valuable than oil in the future. Freshwater is going to be a new gold. Little is known that Israel is manufacturing the most advanced military technology in the world. Presently, China is the top importer of weapons from Israel. Russia is purchasing weapons from Israel. It is Israel that invented drones which were used by NATO in Afghanistan and other countries.

The conflict in Mideast between Muslims would add the already sorry state of affairs of the Ummah. In 2011, there was Arab spring, which was supported by Iran and Muslim Brotherhood. This was culminated in the rise of Dr. Morsi as leader of Egypt but it was a short one. The reason is that Saudi and UAE effectively backed Gen. Sisi's coup, which removed him from power. Remarkably, the coming decades will surely be filled with the story of wrestling between US and resistance forces. The

Arab world is torn apart: one group supports Iranian bloc and the other bloc is loyal to their western masters. USA, which had all the influences in Mideast and would primarily serve as balancing state, can no longer make it. It only shows that America today is different from America ten years ago.

The Great Game in Afghanistan
And the Defeat of US

Taliban appeared a couple of years after the fall of Soviet Russia. It altered the political landscape of Afghanistan when it was tattered, ruined and devastated in postwar era. Two superpowers fought a fierce war in Afghanistan to the death of one empire and one rising and relishing unipolar moment. The battle of Powers and the ensuing civil war between and among Mujahideen factions left the country slide back to the Stone Age. In 2001, US attacked Taliban Government and it fell, collapsed and destabilized. US-led NATO and the coalition of the willing around the world came to assist United States in its alleged war on terror. More than a hundred thousand well-equipped and armed to-the-teeth NATO forces cleared the capital from Taliban. They started the dramatic military adventurism to Afghanistan, which is one of the poorest countries in the world. Taliban forces, on the contrary, were numbered ranging from 30,000 to 60,000 – ill-equipped possessing old model AK47s with no air forces nor tanks and helicopters.

The war has to persist for 20 years. After two decades, US-led coalition of the willing has been on the run. The first incredible humiliation was that US forces left stealthily Bagram Airport in midnight. This was a shameful withdrawal – unprecedented and record-setting.   With this on-and-off war, a tiny oil-rich country was shaking the regional order. Qatar with its Al Jazeera has been introducing a regional order. Qatar is standing between the wars of giants. It has continuously been at the command post behind Turkey and Muslim Brotherhood's military exploits. Qatar was the first country to wrestle Assad Syria. It also operated Libyan politics in post-Qaddafi era. It has been calling civil war-scarred Muslim countries to initiate talks and come to negotiating table. Qatar facilitated talks of conflicting parties in Sudan, Algeria, Tunisia, Libya and Afghanistan among others. Doha used diplomacy to stop war between Hamas and the Zionist state. It is also facilitating the talks between US and Taliban in post-Taliban takeover. Even during the negotiations prior to the withdrawal of the coalition forces, Doha was at the centerfold of the talks. Moreover, Al Jazeera had to cover the Arab Spring 24/7 in 2011. Qatar then was the innocuous sanctuary of Muslim brothers. This tiny country suffered an excruciating and painful sanction of the Arab world but it survived. The reappearance of Taliban signals the end of American empire. Truly, Afghanistan is the graveyard of empires. Greek, Mongol, British, Russian and American empires laid rest in Afghanistan. Post-American Afghanistan sets in motion a new government and a new beginning. This is Afghanistan, which will orbit to Doha's influence. Doha will stay for better and bright new regional order. Qatar may not be independent from western orbit in global stage but at least it is able to stand and sustain neutrality in the face of warring empires such as Russia versus US, Iran versus US and other global powers. Saudi Arabia extended its diplomatic overture to the newly-established Afghan government. Afghanistan is a neighboring country of Iran and that they had bitter past. Saudi

Arabia and Iran had irreconcilable differences from socio-political doctrine to theological position.

Notably, Afghanistan was largely bypassed by modern age. Closed in, mountainous, and desolately poor, it is primarily renowned today for its wealth in military history. The earliest details of Afghanistan come from ancient Greek historians following the exploits of Alexander the Great. After Conquering Greece, Egypt and the Persian Empire with outstanding victories, Alexander's men reached the Hindu Kush. The climate and harsh topography of Afghanistan took Alexander by surprise and his army ran itself ragged fighting the fierce Scythian tribes in the province of Bactria and in Transoxiana, north of Oxus River (Amu Darya). After two years of mobile warfare, during which time an entire 2000-man Greek column was wiped out in an ambush.[95]

Stephen Tanner, in his book, "Wars of the Bushes," described Afghanistan as a transit route of civilizations of the east and west. In the first century, a group called Kushan came off the steppe to create an empire that straddled the great cultures of China, India, Persia and Rome. A Kushan King converted to Buddhism and became responsible for spreading the Great Vehicle or the image of Buddha. During this period the Silk Road started to take shape. Then Kushan fell to Persia and then Persian Sassanid fell to the invading White Huns and then followed by Turks.

In 7th century, Arab Armies conquered the territory. Islam started to take root and with the zeal of the new converts, they launched fierce raids to India extending the borders of Islam. In the succeeding centuries, Afghanistan consolidated its empire and formed one powerful new empire called Khwarezm. In 13th century, the King picked a fight with another rising empire to the east: Mongols. Mongols under the command of Genghis Khan invaded southern Asia establishing a record of destruction that would be unmatched until the World War One. Welding the primitive self-assurance of a nomadic people with ironclad discipline and superb command, Genghis Khan created an army resembled an unstoppable force of nature. The crown prince of Khwarezm, Jalal ad-Din, raised and army and crushed an approaching Mongols.

When European Seafarers directed the flow of commerce to ports, Silk Road dried up. The transportation of business and trade was no longer via land but through seas. The discovery of the New World that would become the focus of commercial energy triggered the European colonialism and that made possible by sea power than marching armies. Then Afghanistan temporarily became isolated, remote and worth no mention in global affairs. Colonialism is an age of European Powers claiming every inch of the globe. Noteworthy powers were France, Russia, Britain, The Netherlands, Belgium, Portugal, Spain and Germany. In Southern Asia where Afghanistan is located, three Powers were at odds with one another: Russia, France and Britain. The elimination then of Napoleon in 1815 left the British Empire and Tsarist Russia as the players of the Great Game, a contest for Southern Asia.

British Empire owned India, the jewel of its empire. When Britain heard that Tsarist Russia appeared in Kabul, it mobilized an army. The fight resulted to the victory of Britain and it governed Afghanistan for a couple of years. Afghanistan to Britain is no more than a buffer state to Russia. The revolt began in the fall of 1841 when an Afghan mob sacked the British residency in Kabul, slaughtering its occupants. The Afghans surrounded the British army while their isolated position became increasingly indefensible. The British army agreed to leave the country. This turned into the most pitiful disaster of the colonial age. Russia did not leave Afghanistan for many decades despite debacles coming one after the other until bipolar moments came. The Cold War became hot war in Afghanistan as the two Superpowers picked a fight for years. United States armed the Mujahideen to fight Russia. The war ended with the victory of Mujahideen. This war did not only isolate Russia from Southern Asia but its ideology would finally join the junkshop of history. Communism started to wane and existed only in antiquity. In 2001, United States invaded Taliban-led Afghanistan for allegedly cuddling Al-Qaeda, which was the primary suspect of the 9/11 attack. The war would persist for two decades. Thousands of US forces died and trillions of dollars were wasted in this war. In 2021, the only Superpower which has policed the world for decades possessing cutting edge weapons would finally leave Afghanistan with a painful heart, grieving and defeated. Taliban 2.0 reclaimed its government. Remarkably, Taliban 2.0 is a new breed of fighters who have learned lessons from their experiences. They learned negotiations, peace talks and diplomacy. They agreed to the political settlement as epitomized by the Doha negotiation. They told the world that they would construct an inclusive government. Women's education is ensured.

With the modern Silk Road constructed only in recent years dubbed Belt and Road Initiatives[96] (BRI) of China, Afghanistan is a significant country. Afghanistan is an important country, aside from its natural resources, to China and that it is always present in a country which is at war with US. With the rise of Taliban 2.0, expectedly, China will recognize it. The new Great Game is in the offing. The Regional Powers would compete over the control of uranium, lithium, etc. These resources-hungry capitalist countries including state-capitalist China would stage unprecedented rivalry. The reason why Mideast and the Muslim world at large has always been the areas of competition of major Powers is clearly described by US State Department in 1944 as: *"the oil resources constitute a stupendous source of strategic power, and one of the greatest material prizes in world history."*[97] More importantly, as Electric Vehicles (EVs) are gradually replacing oil-powered vehicles especially in advanced countries, Afghanistan has a large reserve of lithium, which is the main element of battery – electric vehicles are battery-operated. This only means that Afghanistan will become a hotspot of competition between regional and global powers.

There are two types of US powers: hard and soft powers. Hard power is the military capability of US, which makes it premier in international stage since the death of soviet Russia. In military power, USA has been defeated in many countries including Afghanistan. Another power, which is still operating, is its soft power: the Dollars and the Bretton Woods System. Dollar is still the international monetary unit and IMF and WB are serving the interests of America. There are many approaches the other powers have been enforcing including the establishment of BRICS, SCO and the short-lived MINT (Mexico-Indonesia-Nigeria and Turkey) just to kick US in the stage of prominence. In sum, these organizations were not able to overshadow the power of Bretton Woods Institutions. Iranian revolution cannot go away with this system. It is part of the international systems, which continuously serve America's mission. The Ummah was anticipating a Taliban-led Afghanistan to divorce this system but it was not able to make it. The direction of Taliban government is not different from other Muslim countries.

Development in American Age

There are two opposing development theories namely the Modernization and Dependency theories. Modernization theory is proposed by the western experts living in the developed countries. Accordingly, development is manifested by modern education, high-rise buildings and other big infrastructures. The western countries would try to send aid to the poor countries in order to introduce the culture of modernization. The idea is that development assistance targeted at those particular countries can lead to modernization of their 'traditional' or 'backward' societies. In contrary, dependency theory is an antipodal of modernization theory, which states that poor nations provide natural resources and cheap labor for developed nations, without which developed nations could not have the standard of living they enjoy. Moreover, the western theorists put forth that the rest of the world needs to emulate the development paradigm of the west. Modernization gives birth to enormous number of economic, political and even social schools. It introduced such terms as globalization, democracy, capitalism, free-market economy, rule of law and liberalism to the world. As champion of modernization, the western scientists and thinkers will have to be present to all the countries. Dependency theorists believe on the ideas of emancipation, equality and struggle. They want to get rid of the multinational companies and corporations that kill domestic economy.

To some extent, modern development has been especially seen as an extension of colonialism. Development according to dependency theorists is synonymous with imperialism. In post-independence period, colonialism continued in the context of west controlling the international economic institutions, imposing doctrines like parliamentary democracy and interventions by western dispatched peace-keepers. According to Edward Goldsmith, "the model of development, which has been foisted upon the third world for the last fifty years, is strikingly similar in both aims and outcomes to the imperial colonialism, which preceded it. The aim of development is not to improve the lives of third world citizens but to ensure a market for western goods and services and a source of cheap and raw materials for big corporations. Global development is imperialism without the need for military conquest." Inevitably, there is a perceived problem on the development discourse. One of the main objectives of western countries to realize development is lending money to the developing countries. When a country borrows money for purpose of development, it will be the beginning of sorrow. Once in debt, through IMF, the creditors can institutionalize their control over a debtor country by Structural Adjustment Programs (SAPs), which in effect take over its economy. This loan is sometimes in the form of aid program.

Countries located in a developing path have strategized and design their own respective paradigms. Though the reconstruction of regional paradigms is difficult and challenging, it has to be realized for sole purpose of standing independently away from the orbit of Empire. Gray in his research entitled, 'New Regional Development Paradigms: An Exposition of Place-based Modalities', put forth that invoking the 'regional' development construct in theory and practice is not as straightforward as might first appear. Moreover, Modernization theory of Development as proposed by Emile Durkheim, which is seen as the "Division of Labor in the Society", was very popular. It defined how social order is maintained in society. It also described ways in which primitive societies can make the transition to more advanced society. In retrospect, since the end of World War II, the United States has become a first world power and Americans have put in a lot of effort to construct a new world order based on their mind's eye. Developing countries have become more ill at ease about issues such as colonial rule, European power and this new world order now pay attention to issues related to development. Therefore, traditional development approaches, which have implied a superiority of Europe as well as racist notations, have lost their validity. In post-European world order, America remade the ensuing world order.[98] In Rostow's development model, which then modernization, the focus of this is on economic, social, political or cultural factors. Generally, modernization and dependency theories are two perfectly different theoretical approaches.

Dependency theory was introduced during the 1970s and has been developed into what is called World System Theory. Interesting to note, Rostow identifies five growth stages: (1) The traditional society; (2) The preconditions for take-off; (3) Take-off; (4) The drive to maturity; (5) The age of high mass consumption. To put it in other way, nations will become developed after they undergo series of stages. They must follow the western world to enjoy development and progress. The end result of these stages is the age when a country enjoys full development akin to the stage of the western world. The development discourse during 1980s was dominated by approaches of the middle range. In addition, the concept of modernization theory has its beginning in the classical evolutionary explanation of social change. Emile Durkheim, Karl Marx and Max Weber try to theorize the transformations initiated by the industrial revolution. Development is understood in the capitalist giants as the ability to rise up in the industrial stage. The western model primarily occupies the center-stage and its locus is in the western's partners and allies. It has been quite essential and significant to emphasize that 'western' term is not always geographic. Japan, Australia and New Zealand among other economic powers are now belonged to the caravan of the western countries. In post-conflict development setting, the inevitable predicament of the role of international institutions in rebuilding process emerges and will take its course. Development has been used as conduit to eternal subservience to rich countries. To put it in other way, when a country is bankrupt, it has to borrow from creditor country with interest until the former will not be able to repay such debts to the detriment of its economy. The debtor country will kowtow to the creditor country. On economic bankruptcy, the bankrupt country can bail out but IMF or the lender will see to it that the money is used properly; it has to be supervised.

The birth of United Nations heralded the age of cooperation of all the countries around the world—big or small, weak or powerful countries. The nations of the world had committed to construct a peaceful world after the gruesome world wars. What happened along the way is that many had come forward and said that UN became a de facto colonial office of the Major Powers. They used UN to pursue their foreign policies. Poor countries are drowned in debts and that they live at the mercy of their creditor countries. This set of circumstances put the poor countries in perpetual misery. If only the rich countries would resolve this endless problem, then development is realized in world stage. There are two ways to move forward: the cancellation of the debts of the debtor countries and that the debtor countries should not pay their debts. From there, the world will have to start for a new beginning when all nations will sit in the table of the world equally.

The international economic system changes from time to time. The international economic system began in Bretton Woods Conference, which gave birth to Bretton Woods Institutions such as the IMF and WB. After several decades in postwar era, Washington Consensus[99] emerged and that the aim of its proponent is to design a new model that is stable, equitable and pro-growth. For decades, the Washington Consensus has dominated policy-making yet the global economic order has been slower and inequality risen. But in the end, the policies of Washington Consensus have failed, which facilitated the appearance of Main Street Alternative.[100] This system seeks to modernize the financial architecture. It aims to reduce speculation and make investors invest with an eye to the long term and proper regard to risk.

There is a new development paradigm called regional development paradigm which the developing countries are introducing. According to Concise Oxford English Dictionary, "paradigm" means a model or pattern for something that may be copied and a worldview underlying the theories and methodology of a scientific study. It is a set of theories, assumptions, and ideas that contribute to one's worldview or create the framework from which he operates every day. For instance, one has probably heard the phrase 'The Islamic way of life,' which is a paradigm because it refers to a collection of beliefs and ideas about what it means to be a Muslim.

Moreover, paradigm comprises beliefs and ideas that form a framework to approach and engage with other things or people. Tellingly, "Development Paradigm" is a development model, theories and assumptions. Development paradigm is dynamic and changing. Many theoreticians, politicians, community development workers and even non-government organization (NGO) workers in the world have been tirelessly researching and inventing model to make their respective countries progressive and prosperous. There have been variegated theories emerged discovering ways for development and prosperity. There is old paradigm that countries need to replace and a need to welcome new paradigm becomes important.

Damao cited Gray who opined that the policy field of regional development is perennially faced with new challenges, such as the new global context, which imposes on all countries, regions and firms a reshaping of locational patterns of production, new standards in economic efficiency and innovation capability, and new behaviors in managing technology, production cycles, information and finance. This new global context continues to vex and inspire scholars and practitioners concerned with the development of regions. The old paradigm is fading while the new paradigm, that is, regional development paradigm, is coming especially in the developing countries.[101] Place-based approach even in its early days has been proven effective and efficient. In regional ladder, China was able to use it and it might chiefly be an instrument to its rise as economic power. Ideology-wise, China embraced capitalism but it is state-market economy—not a sort of free-market economy. China is not namby-pamby. In a world of rambunctious cacophony of paradigmatic mayhem, it navigates its own economic potentiality.

Birdsall disclosed that development through strengthening domestic or regional policies for global integration will bear good result. Noticeably, the poorest countries are those least integrated into global markets. The facts are so obvious that most poor developing countries have joined the bandwagon of unilateral trade opening. Industrial countries are highly integrated among themselves but still relatively closed to poor country products and services. Rich countries could significantly ease global inequality by lifting their barriers to imports of agriculture and manufactured textiles.[102]

The self-propelled development of many countries is another symptom that American-created world order is coming to an end. The regional developing countries are waking up and joining the international elite club. The world is not a monopoly of one country which can dictate the rest. Russia and China came forward and introduced their respective models of development away from Washington Consensus. The Ummah can do the same as it has the impeccable development framework taken from the Noble Quran and prophetic tradition. The biggest challenge is lack of unity and unifying position in establishing one Ummah. The politics of divide and rule is still deeply-imbedded in the Muslim world.

Part Four
The Post-American World

"They talk about wanting to re-establish what you could refer to as the Seventh Century Caliphate. This was the world as it was organized 1,200, 1,300 years, in effect, when Islam or Islamic people controlled everything from Portugal and Spain in the West; all through the Mediterranean to North Africa; all of North Africa; the Middle East; up into the Balkans; the Central Asian republics; the southern tip of Russia; a good swath of India; and on around to modern day Indonesia. In one sense from Bali and Jakarta on one end, to Madrid on the other."
-- Former US Vice President Cheney

Chapter Eight

Liberal Capitalism on Declining Trajectory

Capitalism is defined as a system in which property is owned by individuals and that they have absolute freedom unchecked by the state. Capitalism believes in the freedom of ownership and let private ownership raid all elements of production and thereby guarantee the safety of private ownership. This includes the elements of production and other forms of wealth. According to Sadr, the capitalistic doctrine is based on three elements, which constitute its peculiar organic entity that distinguishes it from other doctrinal entities. Firstly, adherence to the principle of private ownership in unlimited form, thus under this doctrine private ownership could not be violated by the state. Secondly, opening the way for every individual to exploit his ownership and possibilities as he likes and allow him to develop his wealth with different means and methods he can. Thirdly, guaranteeing freedom of consumption in the same way as freedom of exploitation is guaranteed.[103]

Political, social, and economic system in which property, including capital assets, is owned and controlled for the most part by private persons. Capitalism contrasts with an earlier economic system, feudalism, in that it is characterized by the purchase of labor for money wages as opposed to the direct labor obtained through custom, duty or command in feudalism. Under capitalism, the price mechanism is used as a signaling system, which allocates resources between uses. The extent to which the price mechanism is used, the degree of competitiveness in markets, and the level of government intervention distinguish exact forms of capitalism.[104]

In relation to the future of liberal capitalism, Fukuyama wrote an interesting article depicting the end of history. Although pantheon of political analysts and experts have questioned and still questioning this notion but in western scholarship, it is seen as guide in understanding the post-communist world. In "The End of History and the Last Man," he opined that in the end of all ideological conflicts, liberalism will triumph over all other rivals and that liberalism is the only ideology that can resolve and address human sufferings and needs. The idea pointed out that all other worldviews and ideologies are bent on putting man to worldly inferno and destruction except liberalism. Liberalism is the peak of human civilizational success. Fukuyama argued that liberal democracy may constitute the endpoint of mankind's ideological evolution and the final form of human government and as such constituted the end of history. This ideology is suited only to the "Last Man." The notion addresses the question of the end of history and the last man who will emerge at the end. The typical citizen of a liberal democracy, which is the last man, gave up prideful belief in his or her own superior worth in favor of comfortable self-preservation. Content with his happiness and unable to feel any sense of shame for being unable to rise above those wants, the last man ceased to be human.[105]

Interestingly, the rise of China has successfully changed the trajectory. The one-party system in China, which is named after the deceased Communism dubbed "Communist Party of China" has emerged as counter-narrative. With all fundamental political earthquakes in the Arab world and Asia, liberalism became problematic. The liberal defenders would defy the current situation to sustain liberalism's future. Muslims, at first, admired liberalism for having established, at least in the west, a humane civilization. But this prestige began to crumble in the last quarter of 19th century. Liberalism was discredited by its explicit complicity with imperialism. Liberalism – and even the neo-liberal ideology – reduced the power of government in favor of private companies and corporation. In China, corporations and companies are state-owned or state-regulated in the least. The political reality in the Philippines and in other parts of South Asia added to the problems of US-led liberal countries. The grip of China has been enabled and consolidated during the rise of President Duterte and military Junta in Myanmar. Starting in 2008 or even earlier, United States was on the verge of economic crisis but it was able to maintain and survive the difficulties. During Trump's presidency US was nearly collapsing as he divorced international institutions and partnerships. He reconstructed America's fate. Subsequently, the most important and dramatic event is the arrival of the Coronavirus. COVID-19 was the turning point of liberalism.

History has a particular explanation on the possibility of the occurrence and recurrence of plague interlacing with the shifting of international power. Plague has an immense role in the destruction of nations and the emergence of other dominating powers. Obviously, during the plague's devastation, leadership, social cohesion and managerial skills of the leaders are tested. The bad and undesirable impacts the plague inflicts are astronomical. It ruins economy, social and nation's ecosystem. It creates political and economic imbalances because of large number of deaths, pressure on leadership and limitation of people's movement. It would, no doubt, affect labor, services, production and the movement of products.

There are two plagues in history that transformed and changed the course of global political history. The first recorded plague or epidemic hit and affected the eastern Roman Empire. It was named Justinian Plague after emperor Justinian I, who was infected but survived through extensive treatment. The pandemic resulted in the deaths of an estimated 25 million to 50 million people.[106] Wazer in her article entitled, "The Plagues That Might Have Brought down the Roman Empire," opined that the Justinian plague was one of the nails in the Roman Empire's coffin and an important milestone in the growth of early Christianity. Quoting Harper, she added that the epidemic undermined the social fabric of pagan society while the orderly response of the Christian community was laid bare. In addition, ancient sources make the Justinian plague sound positively apocalyptic. The people of Constantinople died as such massive rates that an emperor Justinian had to appoint a special officer in charge of coordinating the removal of corpses from the city's streets.[107]

Second disturbing plague, in fact the most dangerous, is the bubonic plague or the so-called "Black Death." Samuel revealed that in the Late Middle Ages, Europe experienced the deadliest disease outbreak in history when the Black Death, the infamous pandemic of bubonic plague, hit in 1347, killing a third of the European human population. Some historians believe that society subsequently became more violent as the mass mortality rate cheapened life and thus increased warfare, crime, popular revolt, waves of flagellants and persecution.[108]

If one has to take a cursory look at the two most devastating plagues, he could see the role they played in the changing international order. The first plague arrived in the 542 C.E. in Constantinople, which was then center of eastern Christianity. The Christian world during this time had been facing internal problems. The most important challenge the Byzantine Empire had been encountering was the reduction of its population. There were economic and political upheavals. In this dramatic situation, another political event to be reckoned with that was to be born was Prophet Muhammad emerging in the center-stage of world politics for less than a century later. The fledgling Islamic movement was able to cripple an empire existing for centuries. That factor worth-considering why empire had succumbed so easily to Islamic conquest is the fact that it was too weak to resist after the heavy damage the plague inflicted decades earlier.

Moreover, the bubonic plague had occurred and served as political watershed. In Europe, much of the transformation that affected European society in the aftershock of the Black Death was born by broader processes that had begun prior to it. The weakening authority of the church was perhaps the most conspicuous of these changes. Evidence suggests that mortality rates were higher than among the general population, possibly because of close interactions among their healthy and sick members. This necessitated a hasty recruitment of church functionaries to refill the depleted ranks. This set of changes could not but erode the overall public standing of the church. The Black Death was destructive for the Byzantine state. It arrived in Anatolia in late 1346 and reached Constantinople in 1347. As in Europe, the Black Death eliminated a significant proportion of the population in the capital and other towns and aggravated the already poor economic and agrarian conditions in cities and the countryside. Years later, the Ottomans would take advantage of this opportunity, when an earthquake that shattered many Byzantine strongholds allowed them to capture the damaged fortress of Gallipoli and advance farther into Byzantine territory.[109] From then on, the Ottomans became major rivals of the Byzantine Empire, whose cities continued to be hit by more natural disasters. By 1453, when Mehmet II conquered Constantinople there was a weak defense.

There are many theories behind the coming of COVID-19 in the open. Conspiracy theories have also been brought out. Others reduced it as a normal disease. Whatever the truth is, one could not hide the undeniable and clear impact the disease has in the collapse of global economy. The disease came when the whole world is waiting for the sunset of American Empire. The unipolar world is coming to its inevitable end. The capitalist economy faced its recession in 2008 and presently it shows no future recovery. The huge domestic and external debt the empire has is significant evidence that it could not reverse the collapsing free market economy.

The State and Capitalism

Signed in 1648, the Treaties of Westphalia brought about an end to the 30-year war (1618–1648) fought between Protestant and Catholic powers in Europe. The commonly held understanding of 'Westphalia' today is that it is an international order marked by 'sovereign, equal, territorial states in which non-intervention into the internal affairs of another state is the rule.[110] As Falk reminds us, however, Westphalia contains an inevitable degree of incoherence by combining the territorial and juridical logic of equality with the geopolitical or hegemonic logic of inequality.[111] Rival states, great powers, and domestic elites frequently breach and circumvent sovereignty and equality when and where it serves their interests to do so.[112] Keene advanced that colonialism and post-colonialism both reified and weakened – at different times and in different places – the establishment of borders. The idea that Westphalia is the harbinger of world 'order' leaves us with the mistaken understanding that it solved a problem of 'anarchy' elsewhere, namely, outside of Europe.[113] For its Euro-centrism and anachronisms many scholars have thus committed to calling 'Westphalia' a myth or narrative that does more to obfuscate the realities of international relations than it does to elucidate them.[114]

Westphalian system has been the model of modern territorial states. The colonial powers used it as a model in carving and drawing the post-colonial states of Asia and Africa. Westphalian model is a pillar or a stake that formed part of international system, which stated that 'state' is a center of international relations. Influential leaders of the Arab world were not able to remove this system since Sykes-Picot Agreement in 1916. The attempt of Islamic State of creating a global caliphate in lieu of territorial state in the Islamic world has failed miserably.

Some scholars have approached the idea that the disappearance of territorial state was facilitated by the rise of globalization. Pantheon of thinkers, professors, experts and political scientists have conceived that globalization is a process in which global economy and political and cultural forces speedily influence the earth and create a new global market, transnational, political and a new global culture. In other words, the globalization is the expansion of the global capitalistic market, the downfall of nation-state, the faster circulation of merchandise, people, information, and cultural models. In brief, moreover, specialists have summarized the traits of the age of globalization with phrases such as the appearance of global electronic village, information revolution, compression of time and space, the termination of geography, and the cybernetic age.[115]

Indeed, Giddens opined that most scholars of globalization have defined their key concept along those lines as a multidimensional set of social processes that create, multiply, stretch, and intensify worldwide social interdependencies and exchanges while at the same time fostering in people a growing awareness of deepening connections between the local and the distant.[116]

At its core, then, Castells advanced that globalization is about the unprecedented compression of time and space as a result of political, economic and cultural change, as well as powerful technological innovations. The slogan 'globalization is happening' implies that we are moving from the modern socio-political order of nation states that gradually emerged in the seventeenth century toward the 'postmodern' condition of globality.[117]

Globalization has rendered the globe akin to a tiny village. The world became a small village where there are fast-paced transactions and that the earth appeared borderless. But it failed to remove the legitimacy of nation-state system and that it continued to exist. There is a suspicion stating that globalization is a special approach to remove the terms colonialism and imperialism in international lexicon. The reality is that globalization is a euphemism of colonization of the capitalist masters.

Many economists have been advancing the idea that economic crisis brought about by Coronavirus is more devastating and worse than the 2008 global financial crisis. US Financial crisis in 2008 had reached global recession. Consequently, this crisis engulfed the entire planet. Then Capitalism was on the brink of collapse. But why is it that capitalism still holds the reins of power after a decade? Definitely, it is different from communism. Communism fell and collapsed in a number of years because its practicality is opposed to a sound mind. In contrary, Capitalism will not fall immediately because it is all-embracing ideology. The financial crisis of 2008, generally, was the result of deep-seated weakness of capitalist system, which carries the seeds of recurring crises. Specifically, the two causes of the crisis among many are the trade deficit and the problem of credit.

Firstly, as for trade deficit, the US imports more goods and services than it exports. For example, the US imported more than 1.6 trillion dollars of goods and services in 2003 while it exported a total of more than 1.2 trillion dollars resulting in a trade deficit of more than 400 billion dollars. The reason of trade deficit is the American consumer's appetite for cheap goods and services imported from Asia especially China and Latin America. In addition, US had a gigantic amount of military spending to wage wars in Mideast and around the world, which raises government expenditure. Secondly, Abdus Salam disclosed that the credit problem materialized in US in the real estate mortgage crisis, after the banks went too far in lending to home buyers between 2002 and 2006, tempting people with low incomes to take out loans by offering them lucrative deals financing 100 percent of home price, which was never done before. One factor that made the small banks even more enthusiastic about recruiting home buyers was the reselling of the mortgage contract as soon as it was done. The small banks sold the mortgages to larger banks such as Lehman Brothers, Bank of America, etc. Other buyers of mortgages were Freddie Mac and Fannie Mae, two companies established by federal government to promote home sales by buying mortgages. These two companies, along with the large banks, issued real-estate-backed securities and sold them to investors such as banks and individuals.[118]

Due to globalized markets and open trading among companies, American-issued real-estate related securities and stocks became popular investments with multinational companies, commercial and central banks, pension funds and individuals.

They all anticipated high profits in the flourishing real estate market of the United States. The market values of real estate property, and thus stocks and securities, soared steadily in US and around the world. Due to this rush to take out loans and mortgages, Federal Reserve gradually raised the interest rate from 1 percent in 2002 to reach the 7 percent in 2006. That scenario brought home buyers face to face with the harsh reality of the deals they signed into and many defaulted on their loans, either because they were not qualified to buy the homes or because of the sharp rise in interest rates, which they could not afford.

The damaging result was that neither home buyers nor banks could benefit from the homes. Billions of dollars were lost on bricks, wood, steel and building materials. The sold homes were mortgaged out to the banks and investment groups. The home buyers were unable to pay back and nobody wanted to buy homes anymore. The American real estate market was dealt a fatal blow. The stocks of lending institutions plummeted and the depositors and investors rushed to withdraw their money. The lending institutions' inability to return money resulted in a devastating financial shock that swept away the largest financial institutions in US and Europe. The credit problem was a spark resulting to a fire that spread out from US to the entire world as a result of globalization.[119]

_____

US-led capitalism is on disintegrating bend. Capitalism, as seen in its history, was not able to solve the problem of poverty, injustice and environmental crisis. Worse, it participates if not the sole responsible to be blamed for the global poverty. More than half of global population is suffering from poverty. Under the aegis of Capitalism, the rich becomes richer and poor, poorer. It does not have heart to remove injustice. It prompts wealth-generation and not on equal distribution of resources. Capitalists created financial and banking system to perpetuate their interests. Stock exchange system is creating financial magic. For instance, 98 percent of the wealth of USA is negotiated in financial market while only 2 percent is the actual goods and services. To make it clear, the actual global production of goods and services is close to 80 trillion dollars a year but the total sum of the same goods and services negotiated in the financial markets is close to 600 or so trillion dollars a year. It means financial markets are nothing but illusory and parasitic.

American leaders and the American people are now grappling with the double-edged sword that is the age of global politics: how to maximize its rewards while minimizing its dangers. In this debate, there is little disagreement over whether the United States should be engaged in world affairs. Both America's extensive global ties and its vulnerability to outside forces make disengagement and isolationism impossible. Nor is there much disagreement on the purpose of American engagement. America's interests are best served by a continually expanding liberal international order, one in which increasing numbers of people share the benefits of open markets and democratic governments.[120] Given the fact that Capitalism is no longer responsive to the world's needs, large numbers of intellectuals are now looking for alternatives. The candidate alternatives are Socialism[121] and Islam.

Chapter Nine
The Great Reset

"The secret of change is to focus all of your energy, not on fighting the old, but on building the new."
Socrates

The Great Reset is a movement within the creative industry to keep hold of the positive environmental shifts that have happened during lockdown and embed these in society as the new normal. "Reset" means to set again or differently. Out of this experience people have the opportunity to "set again" on a grand scale – not because they were forced to, but because they chose to. The world they once knew is not coming back. COVID-19 broke the world open, exposing parts of people's collective reality that needed healing, beyond the pandemic emergency. The result is the realization of a historic tipping point.[122]

Since the ashes of WW2 in 1945, the world was shifting to an international capitalism-based order. Global institutions would replace national unilateralism that caused the world wars; free markets would replace protectionism; and trade barriers and economic prosperity would replace nationalistic trade wars. When the Berlin wall was torn down – beckoning the end of cold war – the forward march of technology, telecommunications and global supply chains from Mexico to Malaysia was meant to break down barriers to global free trade. But now the opposite has happened, instead of nation states shrinking and markets getting bigger, the conflicting situation emerges. Globalization is now under siege for failing to deliver beyond the 1% and state sponsored mercantilism akin to the pre-20th century is now the dominant model of our age.[123] Capitalism is the only existing ideology in the present generation that governs the international system. According to National Intelligence Council, the international system – as constructed following the Second World War – will be almost unrecognizable by 2025. The transfer of global wealth and economic power now under way, roughly from West to East, that is – from US to China, and without precedent in modern history, is the primary factor in the decline of the United States' relative strength. Few countries are poised to have more impact on the world over the next 15-20 years than China.[124]

The ballistic effects of COVID-19 have shaken the international system. Beginning of 2020 marked the outbreak of this dangerous disease originating in China, one that spread worldwide. Consequently, in an increasingly globalized world where the transfer of goods and people is easier than ever before, it is in this way that the virus spared no countries and territories concerned. The World Health Organization[125] (WHO) declared it as pandemic. Pandemic means a disease prevalent over large part of the world. Khan pointed out that most of the world was slow to respond and when they did many

_____

governments responded by implementing travel restrictions, lockdowns and facility closures. The pandemic and subsequent responses have caused global social and economic disruption. The disease produced the largest global recession, since the Great Depression and global famines, affecting almost every section of the world's population. It has led to the postponement or cancellation of sporting, religious, political and cultural events. Schools have also been closed either on a nationwide or local basis in 172 countries, affecting approximately 98% of the world's student population.[126]

The COVID-19 pandemic changed the former world in terms of system, order and values. The world is caught off-guard resulted to unprecedented crisis that knocked the global economy down. It accelerated the transfer of power from US to China. Before the pandemic, China is undeniably overtaking US, albeit slow, in terms of economy and influence around the world, but COVID-19 expedited the march of China reaching a great power status and economic premiership.

World Economic Forum (WEF), which included some of the world's most powerful business leaders and government officials, have announced the reset of the global economy outlining that traditional Capitalism, and the global economy should adopt wealth taxes, additional regulations and a massive Green New Deal-like government program. "Every country, from the United States to China, must participate, and every industry, from oil and gas to tech, must be transformed," wrote Klaus Schwab, the founder and executive chairman of the World Economic Forum. In short, "we need a 'Great Reset' of capitalism."[127] In October 2020, the IMF said similar when its managing director called for a "new Bretton Woods moment."[128] Those behind the Great Reset have decided that Capitalism and Socialism will need to merge. The Great Reset also envisages the COVID-19 crisis as permanent and sees the state and corporations working together to fight the virus. WEF outlined that global leaders will need to steer the market toward fairer outcomes. This means a top-down approach with global corporations and governments steering the global economy and national economies. The Great Reset is already endorsed by the world's largest corporations, G7 governments and global institutes.[129] The post-pandemic world is an important chapter of human history that scholars as well as students of political science, international relations, peace and development must take a look at. Economically, people will witness the emergence of electronic currency system while American power is collapsing. Another ideology would most likely come as alternative in post-capitalist era. The merging of Socialism and Capitalism as epitomized in global leaders' initiatives is orchestrated to save the collapsing capitalism. The combination of capitalism and socialism is clearly demonstrated in China. China has opened its market to outside world but its government is given power to regulate and oversee it. The emerging ideology in post-virus period is akin to Chinese ideology. The meaning of this is that China will chart the future of international system.

Although scholars may differ on whether the turning point from political economy to political science occurred soon after WWII or in the 1970s, it appears safe to assume that such trends and turning points exist; that they affect the plausibility of theories; and that the current coronavirus crisis is creating a situation in which a hitherto less prominent function system – namely, health – will become much more significant. The question, therefore, is whether management and organization theory are well prepared to reflect on rather than just mirror such epochal transitions. Reappraisals of seminal works on bio-politics or bio-power can only be a beginning.[130]

The West's soft power has also been significantly damaged by the pandemic. Far from being China's "Chernobyl," as The Financial Times suggested when the disease first emerged, Asian governments have been swift and decisive in their response to contain the pandemic. In reality, China where the virus originated, was able to contain the virus in months. The edge of China over others – and that one of the main reasons of its successful fight against the virus – is that its political system is highly centralized. With Europe and the US deeply divided and struggling to control the pandemic, this has raised serious concerns about the system of governance in the West. A post-pandemic world will be one with many different powers: China, India, Russia, Europe, Africa, Brazil and the US. Tensions will still exist between and among different countries and global powers. The boundaries of their influence will be contested but there are also significant global problems that can only be managed through close cooperation among them.[131] People need to break with the past and engage with the future that is already upon them. There is no stopping this ongoing Great Reset. But left to its own devices, it will unfold in a stop-and-start, trial-and-error fashion over the course of the next two, maybe three decades. People are hoping that they can move more quickly down the path to real recovery, minimizing the pain and suffering faced by too many, and ushering in a new era of sustainable prosperity for everyone.[132]

The pandemic is a strategic phenomenon that speeded up the rise of the rest especially China and the fall of America. The United States is heading towards a fiscal disaster. It hardly copes up to simultaneously pay for its extensive military involvements around the world; its current commitments to social programs; and the investments in education, infrastructure, and research needed to compete effectively with China and other rivals. If current trends continue, American economic and military dominance will be lost and the era of American empire is over. Whether the U.S. will be succeeded by a new hegemon or the world will enter an era of multiple power centers is as yet uncertain.[133] In Naomi Zack's forthcoming book, The American Tragedy of COVID-19 Social and Political Crises of 2020, she describes the pandemic as a social disaster, by which she means that the disaster is not simply a natural entity or event, but the whole of that event and how it becomes integrated in human society.[134] Viewing the pandemic as a social disaster incorporates more than the lives lost and those sickened by the virus. It also means coming to terms with the way the disaster has reshaped people's understanding of themselves and their world. As Zack explains, "this is what it means to say that disaster is socially constructed – certain changes in society should be viewed as part of a disaster and not merely an effect of a disaster." Disaster can challenge and change people's perspectives on life and the way they engage with each other, and with the world. Indeed, the manner in which a pandemic can do this is captured in a powerful account of the plague presented in Thucydides' History of the Peloponnesian War.[135] As explained above, liberal capitalism is no longer operative and that the world needs a great reset. The liberalization of economy and financial markets in developing countries did not give the results that the Washington Consensus had forecasted. In fact, emerging markets suffered from large capital flights and financial contagion, as demonstrated by the Mexican and Asian crises of the 1990s. Hence, in this critical context, the IMF developed a fourth operational mode: lender of last resort in international crises. For instance, the Fund a couple of years now exerted this function for Greece, Portugal and Ireland.[136] In sum, the IMF supported the American hegemonic order by correcting its deficiencies through four overlapping functions. This is the reason why the Fund is today unable to attentively and critically monitor global affairs. What is to be done? It is clear from its modus operandi that the IMF is afflicted by a lack of universality in its mandate. In a word, the Fund does not represent a place for collective action, but an executive branch of American financial power and its allies. Hence, a reform of the IMF implies reconsidering the reproductive modalities of US power in the era of financialization, in order for this Institution to finally fulfill a truly universal mission.[137] The outcome of the liberalization of economy is clear-cut tragedy as government is left with less function and responsibility. The driving force behind globalization is free-market liberal capitalism. The international companies and super-corporation are free and left unhindered by states wherever they enter for business around the world. Liberalization and global market integration are primary target and the fundamental engine of globalization. The COVID-19 pandemic weakened international capitalism as many countries are rising. The vivid evidence of globalization under siege is China's position in the world.

The post-pandemic era is characterized by the advent of a system between socialism and capitalism or the mixed form. Companies and corporations would still operate and exist but they are checked by government or state. Many people are still unaware that the global shifting of power from West to East - and that the Global North is now in the East specifically China - has just happened. The Great Reset in post-pandemic world that the World Economic Forum has introduced is characterized by the mixed Capitalism and Socialism. It is very clear that the combination of Socialism and Capitalism is seen in the present ideology of China. It is also important to note that the predictions of Fukuyama in his "The End of History" when liberalism will dominate the end of history and that the government or state will have limited power over economy is a false prophesy. The rise of electric vehicles and electronic money will accelerate the death of petrodollars. The world will finally witness the sunset of American Empire.

There are stages towards recovery. The phases of investing for the post-COVID-19 economy will fall into three overlapping periods: preservation, consolidation and innovation. Preservation is the period where uncertainty is so high that the best thing people can do is preserve what they have to see if it provides a useful base for tomorrow. In this phase both investors and governments tend to focus on funding and balance sheet repair. The second phase is consolidation. Here, the companies whose business models fit the moment and are able to demonstrate that they can in fact perform well in a post-pandemic world begin to pull away from the rest. The third phase will be innovation. At the beginning of the innovation phase, not all aspects of the post COVID-19 world will be clear, but they will become so. Companies and customers will now have a clearer grasp of their new needs and the nature of what they expect in a new vendor or product.[138]

Chapter Ten
The Rise of the Digital World

The coronavirus was able to change the course of history as it facilitated the rise of other powers while exposing the weaknesses of our civilization and many government systems. It has a big impact on economic and political balance. It is true that the virus had started in China but it was able to contain it and that it handled the virus crisis effectively. Viewing the last two decades the world's geo-economic axis has been moving from North to the Global South. India and China have been en route to economic success before the arrival of the virus. The COVID-19 has hit them so badly but they were able to prevent it from totally destroying their economy.

The said "Wealth Shift" from the North to the South was justified by the World Bank. The rise of China and India, the emergence of BRICS, the appearance of collective financial statecraft, as embodied in newly created international financial institutions like the Asian Investment and Infrastructure Bank (AIIB) and the New Development Bank, all point in the direction of a major international shift.[139] These institutions served as counterweight to the International Monetary Fund (IMF), which is a US-dominated financial system. A variety of initiatives including the establishment of the New Development Bank, led several analysts to view the BRICS as a potential driver for parallel order.[140]

On international relations, the coming of the virus has a major impact on the practice of diplomacy. Diplomats made use of digital technologies before the crisis but in rather amateur and half-hearted way. Suddenly, the risk of contagion meant that diplomats and statesmen could not meet face to face. Summits and conferences had to be held by video-conferencing.[141] The digitalization of diplomacy was accelerated but the core of diplomacy remained the same and even now, it had to be expressed through digital channels. Conferences and summits, which are normally conducted in face-to-face become online activities. Meetings of world powers such as G7, G20, WEF and UN General Assembly suddenly turned online. The Speeches of the different heads of states in 2020 UN General Assembly were made possible through online platform.

Technology is a peak of human invention and intellectual development. The rise of internet-based transaction has speeded up new system. The invention of Radio, Television and Cinema among others was an opportunity in spreading knowledge and information. The fast progress in the field of technology, mainly the invention of the computers and the Internet, has ended up in a new era, namely the Information Age (IA). The advanced pieces of information and communication technologies (ICTs) have facilitated and accelerated the processing and dissemination of knowledge throughout the world, meanwhile creating a huge network coverage that also took the globalization and intercultural communication (IC) to an upgraded dimension. IC has been a hot issue for a considerable time that has increased its importance during the last three decades.[142] In the early days of the internet, it was possible to order products and services for delivery offline. Later it became possible to order those same goods and services for delivery online especially during the pandemic. It is possible even to consume those goods and services online. Pandemic is a norm-setting phenomenon, which popularized physical distancing. Physical distancing is a strategy and measures to prevent the spread of the virus. It means that people will no longer work face-to-face because online activity becomes the new normal. COVID-19 has fast-tracked the realization of a digital world. Electronic activities in relation to office works, education, business, governance and economy have carried the day and that e-transaction will dominate the future. In office works, activities, reports and communications are done through electronic means. Meetings are no longer conducted in face-to-face manner but through different online platforms such as Zoom, Teams, Google Meet, Skype, among others.

During the lockdowns, the delivery of education is affected. The arrival of the pandemic was unexpected and that there was no government preparation. The face-to-face classes were suspended all of a sudden that gave way to other learning platforms: online classes and distant modular classes. Modular classes were introduced to education system. This learning system and modality has inevitable effects on the teaching-learning process. Despite negative effects of modular classes to the students' learning, this learning modality has also offered opportunity.[143] Online classes are implemented especially in big cities with access to internet. The pandemic had truly triggered an unprecedented disruption in education. According to UNESCO, after several months, more than 1 billion students – more than 60 percent of the children worldwide who were enrolled in school – are directly affected by nationwide school closures.[144]

On business, Amazon, Facebook, Apple, Google and other online shopping platforms benefited from the online trading. People would just click their cellphones' keypad to buy products and goods and their orders arrive at their doorsteps. Online marketing became the means of business. The Markets are right on everyone's fingertips. In the parlance of governance, public administration and governance go online. The office memoranda and orders are posted on Facebook, e-mails and other online platforms. Executive Meetings would be conducted online. Submission of reports and even conducting researches are done through online. Practically, all office transactions and activities are online. We found ourselves existing in the digital universe and it seems, we are adapting well, at least now.

Chapter Eleven

The Sunset of Petrodollars and the Sunrise of Electronic Money

US became the superpower because it was able to use the situation on its favor. In 1945, that is after the world wars, having the world's largest gold reserves at the time, the US remodeled the global financial system around the dollar. The new system, created at Bretton Woods, tied the currencies of every country in the world to the US dollar through a fixed exchange rate. It tied the US dollar to gold at a fixed rate of $35 an ounce. This made the dollar as good as gold. The Bretton Woods system made the US dollar not only a world's premier reserve currency.[145] It effectively forced other countries to store dollars in their respective national banks for international trade and business, or to exchange with the US government for gold. Being the issuer of the global reserve currency guaranteed international demand for the dollar. This meant the US could print dollars unlimitedly since the wider world always needed dollars and would absorb the ensuing inflation. The USD was made a universal currency and a standard unit of measurement. The defeat of American empire in Vietnam War resulted in the US printing large amount of dollars than it could back with gold. In the last quarter of 1960s, dollars circulating had increased relative to the amount of gold backing them. This motivated foreign countries to exchange their dollars for gold resulted to the draining of US gold supply. President Nixon temporarily suspended the convertibility of Dollar to gold in 1971. This is still in effect at present. Henry Kissinger went to negotiate with Saudi Arabia. He demanded the Saudi Government to trade oil with dollars. The agreement was Saudi, being the largest producer of oil, should not trade it with any other currency except dollar. They agreed and petro-dollar system was born. Later, oil would be so abundant in Saudi Arabia while dollars would be printed out of the thin air. Oil in the Arab world turned out to be a mountain of gold. The coming of dollars in the center of global economy catapulted USA to the pulpit of premiership. In return, US had to protect Saudi government from any foreign enemy.

The idea of green energy and the rise of digital world have threatened the very existence of petrodollars. China championed the manufacturing of electric vehicle in compliance with the green economy. Norway projected that in 2025, all cars and vehicles would be electric-powered. The world is going to the direction of post-oil era to the death of petrodollar system. In the wake of the petrodollar dominance, another system is dawning, the electronic money system. Through electronic money, the world will be governed by another nation which will use it as its weapon. Dr. Imran Hosein named the state of Israel as the next ruling state in post-American world. The emergence is beyond proposal but a grand plan.

Indeed, one of the most important elements of electronic world is the emergence of electronic money. One feature that distinguishes electronic money, however, is that, like traveler's checks, the values being transferred need not represent the liabilities of private depository institutions. Both banks and nonbanks have experimented with providing these payments services. Value originates in a stored-value when the card owner pays the provider some form of money to fuel the card. After that, an exchange of electrons between the memories of two persons' cards conveys information needed to effect a payment.[146] *E-money is the newest instrument in the payment system, and according to one broader definition this is the money that is transferred electronically. But still, the definition of e-money is more complex and it is a problem to describe a dynamic phenomenon within a comparatively static framework.*[147] Thirty years ago, people could not imagine that the world would be opened before them just with the click on the mouse, so, with this experience they could expect that the world would be covered with e-money transactions in the future.[148]

The crypto-currency concept was introduced 46 days after the bankruptcy of the Lehman Brothers, the event marking the beginning of the second biggest financial crisis in the human history.[149] A crypto-currency is a digital asset designed to work as a medium of exchange using cryptography to secure transactions, to control the creation of additional value units, and to verify the transfer of assets.[150] Crypto currencies including Litecoin, Bitcoin, Libra and Ethereum became popular in international trade and business transactions.

The rise of crypto-currencies poses an existential threat to many traditional functions in finance. Crypto-currencies embrace a peer-to-peer mechanism and effectively eliminate the middle man, which could be financial institution. For example, no bank account or credit card is needed to transact in the world of crypto-currencies. Indeed, a crypto-currency wallet serves the same function as a bank vault. With a smart phone and the internet, the potential exists for a revolution in financial inclusion given that over two billion people are unbanked.[151] However, people need to have access to smartphones, internet connectivity and technology literate to achieve inclusion or else, this will create an added barriers for inclusion especially in developing countries. According to the European directive, e-money presents a monetary value, as represented by a claim on the issuer, which is stored on an electronic device, issued upon receipt of funds in an amount not less in value than the monetary value issued and accepted as a means of payment by undertaking other than the issuer. When individuals stored their cash in banks, it transformed, in their view, into a digital form. In addition to cash in circulation, broad money includes digitally represented money.[152] E-money may be granted a higher status than cash as ICT advances. Nonetheless, money, as a representative form of a quantifiable and tradable value, has transformed from a physical representation of bullion to a digital record kept at trusted institutions. During this transformation, e-money has become more convenient and has reached a broader group of users. Money is already electronic.[153]

Before the pandemic, Bitcoin and other crypto-currencies are appearing in place of the deteriorating dollars. The Bitcoin community is striving to push into the mainstream through innovation and solving old problems. Other forms of crypto-currency have already emerged and have gained followings of their own, and each slightly different from Bitcoin and arguably valid. Some nations like Iceland have even begun to start their own national crypto-currencies.[154] Bitcoin will always have a difficult time competing with these household names. PayPal has been very successful as the eBay exchanging system, and could potentially be moved into mobile payment. Companies like Apple, Google, and Amazon have entire marketing budgets with a foothold in the mobile application market, giving them a huge advantage over Bitcoin's comparatively small-time players. Mobile consumers want to be able to buy things with phones directly, and Bitcoin would have a hard time rallying together as a community to beat out competitors.

Digital, crypto and electronic currencies became popular and prevalent as alternative to paper money. Those countries which suffer from the US sanctions and inflations opted to use crypto-currencies in order to save their worsening financial crisis. Scholars connected the irreversible fall of dollars with the emergence of the COVID-19 pandemic. In the early part of 2020, the world experienced lockdowns and restrictions. The demand for oil fell to such an extent that tourism, oil companies, transport industry were angst-ridden because of movement and travel restrictions including the reduction of face-to-face transactions. Flights were cancelled and land transportations were limited. The oil demand had plunged sharply in global market and that it had enormous effects to the dollar activity. Oil as being traded in US dollar, in connection, the supply level of oil was drastically reduced after the coming of the virus and surely it would not come back to its pre-pandemic levels.

The notion of reduction of CO_2 emission, which has been a global concern and the incidental fall of demand for oil because of COVID-19 restrictions, facilitates the massive production of electronic vehicles. The world is heading to mass production and manufacturing of electric vehicles as alternative to oil-run vehicles as a mechanism for climate change mitigation. Global warming has been on constant rise because of the massive CO_2 emissions brought about by burning of fuels such as oil and diesel. This across-the-board oil combustion results to high concentration of gas and carbon dioxide in the atmosphere, which ultimately quickens climate change process.

For the most benefit, electric vehicle deployment requires four concurrent strategies: (a) electrification of vehicles; (b) provision of sufficient charging equipment; (c) de-carbonization of the electricity generation; and, (d) integration of electric vehicles into the grid. In the end, benefits of Electric Vehicles include zero tailpipe emissions and therefore less local air pollution and, depending on the power generation, lower CO2 emissions. EVs can also reduce noise pollution in cities. Governments should also consider promoting electric two-wheelers and electric buses as a way of reducing pollution and noise in highly-populated regions where point-to-point charging is possible.[155] In the 21st century, EVs have seen resurgence due to technological developments, and an increased focus on renewable energy and the potential reduction of transportation's impact on climate change and other environmental issues. Project Drawdown describes electric vehicles as one of the 100 best contemporary solutions for addressing climate change.[156]

Despite one of the goals of electric vehicle adoption being to limit the carbon footprint and pollution caused by internal combustion of engine vehicles, a rising concern among environmentalists is the manufacturing process of electric vehicle batteries. In current practice, these vehicle batteries rely heavily on the mining industry of rare earth metals such as cobalt, nickel, and copper.[157]

According to 2018 study the supplies of mined metals would need to increase 87,000% by 2060 globally for transition to battery-powered EVs. Rare-earth metals such as neodymium and dysprosium and other mined metals such as copper, nickel and iron are used by EV motors, while lithium, cobalt, manganese are used by the batteries.[158] Of all the oil consumed in the U.S., 70 percent is used for transportation. Further, passenger vehicles use 70 percent of transportation oil. Globally, a rising middle class in China and India is causing demand for passenger cars to balloon, and with it, demand for oil. By 2050, there may be as many as 1.5 billion cars on the road, compared to 750 million in 2010.[159]

Electric car and electronic money will hasten the death of the dying empire. As mentioned beforehand, United States became a superpower after World War II, because it had controlled monetary system and US dollars became the international currency unit. After Vietnam War, US and Saudi Arabia agreed to trade oil with dollars, this led to US dollars to become global currency reserve. Oil industry turned out to be the most valuable goods around the world. Manufacturing of millions of oil-powered vehicles put dollars to the center-stage. Later, US dollars were used in numerous international transactions even though they had nothing to do with American business. Through dollars, America ruled the world.

The tiny virus has suddenly cut down the power of the mighty dollars. Electronic money system will appear in post-pandemic world. Online businesses have been teeming during pandemic. Payments in many different business transactions are now pure e-money. From book publishing to purchasing of plane ticket and from attending classes to sending proposals have all become online. In the coming decades, dollars or the paper currency in general will become irrelevant. Moreover, the mass production of liquid-fueled vehicles, which had catapulted oil to top global product in the end benefited US and that it became the leading state in the world, will be considerably reduced as the rechargeable vehicles will become popular in post American world. There is no forever in the love-story of Oil and Dollars. In extension, the commitment of a hundred countries of zero carbon emissions in 2050 is another factor of how oil ends its supreme role in global economy and politics.

Besides, since the Diesel-gate scandal in 2015, the share of diesel vehicles in new car registrations in Europe has fallen from 52% in 2015 to less than 30% currently. Several European cities have announced that they will ban diesel cars from inner cities, including Oslo, Paris, Rome, Hamburg and Madrid, from 2024. Many other cities announced a similar ban starting between 2025 and 2030. According to Bloomberg, a total of 24 European cities with population of more than 60 million are banning diesel engine cars over the next decade.[160] Therefore, the post-COVID-19 age is described as the end of petrodollars and the rise of electric vehicles will simultaneously facilitate the emergence of international electronic money system.

Chapter Twelve
The Future Prospects and Challenges

This emergent 'great power competition' narrative has created new uncertainties for international security, not least for the use of remote warfare as a tactical tool for states. But there are reasons to be doubtful that it will mark the end for remote warfare or a return to large-scale interventions. In the 'great power competition' era, states such as the US will rely heavily on partnerships. As Watts, Biegon and Mahanty noted that security cooperation will likely remain an important tool in the American foreign policy. This will likely be true in the case of its allies too. Several countries are considering following a light-footprint strategy of 'persistent engagement,' where a state 'maintains a presence in a country, with few troops, and work with regional and local partners to try and build influence and knowledge.'[161]

The global economy took massive hit in 2020 as lockdowns and restrictions across the world took national economies off-line for months. The impact was incredibly broad and deep. It adversely affected mobilization, manufacturing, GDP and employment. The global economy was due a recession in 2020, but the COVID-19 pandemic put global economy into a crisis worse than the 1930s global recession. In addition, the superpower is facing national and domestic challenges. It maintains its global reach that costs big amount of dollars that cause American crisis. The economic inequality and racial discrimination divided American people. The black-white and red-blue divide shook the very foundation of America.

In 1979 Egypt, headed by President Sadat, formally recognized the Zionist entity in a formal treaty. It took another decade for Jordan to do the same. It then took a quarter of a century for the next nations to recognize Israel and establish normal relations. The recognition of the Zionist entity by UAE, Bahrain, Sudan and Morocco was under the aegis of Trump. The normalization between the Arab states and Israel would contribute to the damage of Palestinian revolution. Israel could tell the world that its existence is legitimate because of Arab recognition and probably other Arab and Muslim countries would follow suit. Palestine is left and abandoned by its supposed protectors. The idea of realizing a two-state-solution in the present setting becomes next to impossible.

Global Injustice

COVID-19 exposed the wealth inequality. The inequality has been witnessed by the world even in the distribution of vaccines and access to quality health care services. Capitalist and wealthy countries manipulated and controlled the in-flow of vaccines to the underdeveloped countries. Though there was inequality brought about by capitalism prior to the coming of pandemic, it has aggravated this problem. Poor countries mainly the Muslim world is suffering from this inequality and injustice. Syria and Yemen have been especially undergoing humanitarian crisis. Aside from the endless wars, there are times that humanitarian assistance is blocked by the competing regional powers.

The greatest injustice committed against the Islamic world is the treatment to the Palestinians, Kashmiris, Rohingyas, Uighurs and other minority Muslim groups around the world. It is so clear in the UN charter that any minority group has a fundamental right to establish its own government reflective with its culture and tradition. There is colossal evidence of this injustice. There are many island states in the map, which are given freedom by United Nations, but why is it so hard for Palestine? The challenge in post-American world is that the occupation of Palestine will continue at all cost. With the normalization between Israel and the Arab states, there is a possibility that Israel will become leading state in Mideast.

Injustice in world stage infiltrates political, economic, social and cultural infrastructures. The political system of UN is in reality undemocratic. The five members of the Security Council, i.e. US, UK, France, China and Russia, have weaponized their veto powers, which results to manipulating the international system. The UN General Assembly has been puny in the face of dictatorial tendency of the Security Council. When it comes to voting resolution, US, UK and France have been all-time on advantageous position. They have large number of overseas territories which are just dots in the map but considered independent states and that counted as they counted big countries such as Russia and China. Vatican, Nauru, Monaco, Tuvalu, Marshall Islands, Saint Kitts and Nevis, Malta, Grenada, the newly-independent Barbados among many small countries which joined the ranks of nations, their populations are just a few thousands. Bangsamoro, Kashmir, and Palestine have far exceeded these independent countries in terms of populations and territories but they are still crying for independence. The main reason is that their call for independent states does not enjoy backing of the major powers.

On economic line, the international capitalism is introduced as international ideology in order that foreign powers could infiltrate all countries of the world. McDonald, Marlboro, Coca Cola are among the US companies penetrated all countries through the canon of capitalism imposed on humanity. The states are found weak in the face of transnational corporations and that they have fettered hands to regulate them. The Global North is in luxury enjoying world's wealth coming from the Global South. The mining companies, which exploit natural resources of the poor countries, would no doubt leave them in perpetual misery. These companies pay cheap labor and services to the community dwellers while extracting the natural resources and perpetuating bad labor practices. Wealthy countries process the raw materials and then produce finished products. The products are sold in global market. In short, the rich countries would simply steal the wealth of the poor countries – these poor countries do not receive benefits from their resources except for some but not enough to compensate the damages that the relationships have caused. The rich countries also infiltrate the poor countries through development aid. The aid can be in the form of human resource development such as scholarships and foreign studies.

On Social affairs, the western powers were able to turn humanity as their carbon copies. Islam has been the promoter of just society and governance. Islam recognized built-in differences of mankind but not gender-related such as legalization of homosexuality, wherein man can marry another man. Islam also puts women on high station but there are situations when women are not allowed to enjoy because of physical security and emotional considerations. For instance, if a girl wants to have economic freedom by earning a living through prostitution, Islam would not allow such, because that will be an erosion of morality and damage to her reputation. In some instances, women cannot lead a nation or a religious leadership, not because they lack the virtue and honor, but to protect them from risky responsibilities and also to promote equity based on their honor and nature. Some reasons are based on the biological make-up of the woman, which makes their emotions unstable due to many hormonal and systemic disturbances. Another is the cultural and religious norm, being the light of the family, the first teachers of their children and their caregiving responsibilities to her family.

The culture of Islam is that women have and are given a limited power in the Islamic society. They need to cover their body to avoid temptations. Western countries have initiated women empowerment and gender equality. There is no problem about gender equality and women empowerment on the first level but not outstepping the red line.

The Shifting of Power

With the rise of China, many have for long considered global power ebbing away from the west who dominated the globe for the best part of 500 years to the Far East. While economic power was already moving East, the COVID-19 pandemic has seen a growing admiration for the East Asian response.[162] US will definitely fall because of many factors mentioned above. China and Russia will once again enjoy relative power and strength. In post-pandemic, the world will witness the power transfer from US to the rest. Many countries suffer from COVID-19 but not China. China's economy rose and is slowly taking over the global market and global power.

The alliance of Russia and China emboldened other regional powers to join the alliance. Iran, Pakistan and other regional powers have been preparing to join the China-Russia alliance. Russia took central Asia from American influence while China invited Iran to the SCO. In post-virus years, America will no longer enjoy its unipolar moment as the regional powers are rising.

At the 2019 Second Belt and Road Forum, President Xi proclaimed that the BRI "has opened up new space for economic growth, produced new platforms for international trade and investment and offered new ways for improving global economic governance."[163] The declared goals of the Digital Silk Road include constructing and strengthening internet infrastructure, improving communication connectivity, enhancing cyber-security, promoting e-commerce, and developing common technology standards.[164] Additionally, four port projects in particular have been flagged by Chinese strategists as potential strategic strongpoint sites in the Indo-Pacific and are worth examining. Each one is at a diverse stage of development, including in terms of potential military functionality. They are Pakistan's Gwadar Port, Cambodia's Koh Kong Port, Sri Lanka's Hambantota Port, and Myanmar's Kyaukphyu Port. Both Pakistan's Gwadar Port and Sri Lanka's Hambantota Port are situated along China's maritime lifeline stretching through the Indian Ocean to the Middle East. Gwadar sits at the mouth of the Persian Gulf and Hambantota is located on one of the world's busiest shipping routes in the Indian Ocean. Myanmar's Kyaukphyu Port and Cambodia's Koh Kong Port are in close proximity to the Malacca Strait, a critical maritime chokepoint and security concern for China. All four meet the strategic strongpoint criteria of geostrategic importance.[165]

Another story is China's COVID-19 "facemask diplomacy." It represents a deliberate exercise in soft power. While it backfired in some places, it is noteworthy that much of the aid was directed to BRI countries and that Chinese state media branded it as a new turning point in building the Health Silk Road.[166] Beijing sent planes filled with thousands of test kits and hundreds of thousands of facemasks to major cities throughout Pakistan.[167] Hundreds of thousands of test kits and personal protective equipment items were sent to the Philippines, Cambodia, and Myanmar, in some cases along with a medical team.[168] China agreed to extend $500 million in financial assistance to Sri Lanka along with donated masks and test kits.[169] And while Chinese requests for public praise as a quid pro quo for humanitarian donations backfired in some places, government officials in these countries were effusive in their thanks.[170]

As America is suffering, the Biden's Build Back Better Act was enacted to systematize a mechanism that would serve as counterweight to the Belt and Road Initiatives of China. The BBBB will be the most transformative investment in children and caregiving in generations. It is the largest effort to combat climate change in American history. It has the biggest expansion of affordable health care coverage in a decade. It is the most significant effort to bring down costs and strengthen the middle class in generations. It is fully paid for and will reduce the deficit by making sure that large, profitable corporations cannot zero out their tax bills. It will no longer be rewarding corporations that shift jobs and profits overseas, asking more from millionaires and billionaires, and stopping rich Americans from cheating on their tax bills. As the world is leaving the unipolar moment, regional powers including Muslim countries will join the Club of the Powers. Iran, Pakistan, Saudi Arabia, Qatar, Turkey and UAE are potential candidates for regional powers. Qatar and UAE are small countries, which are adored of their military, political and economic power. Qatar is located between the western camp and the Ummah camp. Ummah camp is an imaginary camp where collective interests of all the Muslims are secured. In reality, there is no Ummah existing now but in principle, all Muslim countries belong to one Ummah. Moreover, Qatar has been truly inseparable with Turkey. They were influenced by the ideology of Muslim Brotherhood. UAE and Saudi Arabia are friends and allies for so long and they have solid connection. These two countries are allies of the western world. Pakistan is a nuclear power. Unlike with the other Muslim countries, it has a never-ending conflict with non-Muslim country, India. India and Pakistan are both potent countries considering their national powers in terms of geography and population.

Iran is the leading state of Shia branch of Islam and an heir of Safavid Empire. It has a considerable degree of sway to some countries in Mideast. Saudi Arabia, which is the leading state of Sunni Islam, is in conflict with Iran. Their proxies have been fighting in the ground. Their conflict manifested in Syria, Yemen, Iraq and Lebanon. They are on collision path. Surely, their interests could not be reconciled. This means disunity of the Ummah will stay in the future and this is the biggest challenge confronting the Muslim world. While Russia, China and US would compete over the natural resources of Mideast, regional powers would also join the competition. Furthermore, while the former unchallenged power and influence of US are ending, every regional power would have its respective policies and systems to enforce. US could no longer bomb any country which is not democratic. Every country would re-invent its national policies and systems without constant international pressure. Basing the argument on the above, Israel would finally rise as a power alongside Russia, China, Iran, Pakistan and other potential regional powers. Israel would become a powerful country alongside others in post-unipolar world. Simultaneous with the collapse of American empire is the rise of Israel.

Islam and Climate Change

Islam asserts the need to believe in God. It is God-centered faith. It is also a worldview. Worldview states and differentiates good and bad. Prophets, the bearers of God's messages and commandments, were sent to people in different time and in numerous circumstances and spaces to call them to the path of enlightenment and knowledge. God wanted His people to believe Him and follow His commands for the good of the society and then civilizations were born. Prophet Musa (Moses) was sent to the children of Israel to inform them of the commands of God and to establish a nation free from the oppression of Pharaoh. He was the embodiment of opposition to pharaonic age. In the same way, Prophet Isa (Jesus Christ) led the Children of Israel to the path of God but many of them were found averse to this direction. At last, Prophet Muhammad was sent for the last time to call humanity for deliverance and that it signaled the end of time but many opposed him.

Years became centuries in post-Islamic period when science turned out to be a powerful weapon against religion. Charles Darwin was an erstwhile seminarian but upon learning science blindly, he started to question religion and creation and that he theorized that man is the last stage of the evolutionary ladder. All things must have come from single cell. This cell evolved. A horse must have come from chicken and man from monkey so on and so forth. Science, in other words, prioritizes knowledge that is proven, evidenced and clear. "To see is to believe" is the foundation of experiment and scientific investigation.

Thinkers and philosophers went beyond the mere debate between religion and science as they crafted and theorized philosophies and ideologies that run contrary to God. Then many politico-ideological lexicons appeared such as capitalism, communism, democracy and secularism. These are all bent to remove religion from public and social affairs and that religion should be cocooned to personal life.

Interestingly, based on the development of science, the world is returning back to the fold of religion and the remarriage of the former and the latter is inevitable. Physics is stepping further miles and farther than people expected. At present, many scientific discoveries and hypotheses prove the existence of higher world. The relativity of time proves the different layers and dimension of time, which prophet Muhammad and Prophet Isa had been telling humanity 1400 and 2000 years ago respectively. The light and energy can be explained by physics. Scientists proved that they are beyond matter. The discovery of Black Hole proves that there are many adventures that science has to trek while religion specifically Islam has it thousands of years ago. Mystics or those who acquired higher knowledge believe that the dead people have still connection with the living people on earth. Science today speaks of the possibility of energy left by dead person and that only the lifeless body is gone not the energy. In other words, Science is discovering the mysteries of time, space, distance, light and energy while Islam has thoroughly explained them a thousand of years ago.

Scientists have methodically examined and investigated environment to such an extent that Europe had produced pool of scientists, who conducted many experiments. However, one result of the misplaced science is the idea of "experiment." Islam does not in any way run contrary to science. In fact, science was flourishing in Islamic world during Abbasid and Andalusian empires. The conflict between the true science and false science is that the latter would put forth that everything that cannot be proved by experiment is not true. This is not always true especially that religion believes on the existence of metaphysical world. This idea crept in epistemology. Eventually, knowledge has been deeply secularized. The rise of science, especially the false one, in Europe was the fall of Islam in world stage. Europe quickened industrial revolution. Afterwards, European Powers flocked to different Asian and African countries in search of natural resources.

Talking about Climate Change, one can start by discussing environment and nature. Environment or the Mother Nature is the source of people's livelihood, food, water, shelter and all basic human needs to live in dignity and generally for their survival. Trees provide human beings oxygen that is of great help for their existence. It is a protection against deadly storms and scorching sun. Technology flourishes out of Mother Nature; petroleum is a gift of nature. Oil facilitated the booming global economy. Nasr wrote, "Our need for nature is not only to feed and shelter our physical bodies, but also and above all to nurture our souls. As the complement to the Qur'an as revelation, nature responds to our spiritual needs."[171]

The problem starts on the inordinate and unwarranted exploitation of the natural resources. Mountains are now devoid of green forest because of voracious and intentional cutting of trees in large volumes. Trees that give people fresh air and oxygen and catch carbon dioxide are ominously exhausted. The result is that nothing will now catch that carbon dioxide in the air resulting to global warming. In addition, the atmosphere is filled with toxic gas. The carbon dioxide, nitrous oxide, methane and other toxic materials by the flourishing companies and factories are hovering over the atmosphere which impact climate change. Climate change is the biggest problem besetting humanity. Catastrophic storms and extreme weather conditions regularly hit many countries claiming heavy tolls and inflicting destruction each year passing. Humanity is under siege. Without resolving this gargantuan and head-cracking dilemma will potentially cause massive destruction and extreme poverty and human sufferings. The Holy Quran has warned humanity, it says: "Mischief has appeared on land and sea because of that the hands of men have earned that (God) may give them a taste of some of their deeds: in order that they may turn back (from Evil)."[172]

Of additional concern is the fact that CO2 is being emitted at an increasing rate, thus indicating that not only are we travelling in the opposite direction to that which we need to be going in, but that this pace is accelerating. The net effect as predicted by the Intergovernmental Panel on Climate Change (IPCC) is a potential warming of up to 1.4°C to 5.8°C by 2100.[173] However, temperatures over land are predicted to rise even further to between 3°C and 8°C.[174] This situation the world is in happens not by chance. It has a connection with the international ideology and belief system. The rise of capitalism as ideology commenced global competition and rivalry resulted to the age of exploration and then the European colonialism. Industrial revolution accelerated the destruction of forest and the environment in general. European powers explored the globe seeking for raw materials and riches. Asia, Africa, Americas and the Fareast became and arena of competition. The discovery of petroleum speeded up the manufacturing of vehicles. While Europe was on the age of development, the Muslim world was on the valley of backwardness. The engine of European development was the Islamic lands. In post-European lordship, the Muslim world was an important colony of America. This was the peak of capitalism. Enshrined in the unwritten rule of capitalism is the rivalry of Great Powers over the natural resources of the world. The emergence of hundreds of companies, factories and manufacturing corporations

---

exacerbated the air and water pollutions. Toxic materials dominated the atmosphere while trees were removed from forests.

In terms of historical emissions, industrialized countries account for around 80% of the carbon dioxide build-up in the atmosphere to date. Since 1950, the US has emitted a cumulative total of roughly 50.7 billion tons of carbon, while China (4.6 times more populous) and India (3.5 times more populous) have emitted only 15.7 and 4.2 billion tons respectively. Annually, more than 60% of global industrial carbon dioxide emissions originate in industrialized countries, where only about 20% of the world's population resides.[175]

After years and decades, the world's biggest problem is climate change. Countries around the world have offered so many solutions. UN would conduct summit yearly to find out environmental sustainability. The developed countries, which are primarily accountable for environmental degradation, are at the front position in hunting for solution. The ultimate solution to this world crisis is to take a look at its very root. The very root is the capitalism itself, which legitimized massive competition to the destruction of the environment.

There are two solutions in order to mitigate this fatal crisis. First solution is political and the second one is social. Politically, United Nations, as family of nations, should have a political will. It has to impose policies, rules and regulations that members-states abide by and those who refuse to follow among them should necessarily be sanctioned. Companies and factories in different parts of the world should be UN-regulated. In so doing, manufacturing companies can now regulate the emission of carbon dioxide. Socially, capitalists should be humane enough considering the effects of their companies, factories and corporations. Countries should reduce the use of plastics and avoid the burning of poisonous and toxic materials to lessen the effects of climate change. The least that any human being can do in mitigating the situation is to manage waste responsibly. The time is ticking. Humanity is facing a dangerous future. As Oius articulates, Muslims must condemn and act against multinational corporations and regimes destroying nature in addition to the cynical economic system. One way of undertaking such action would perhaps be to join the emerging global movements and networks demanding economic and environmental justice, as long as these movements act according to Islamic and democratic principles.[176]

Another solution is Green Economy introduced by United Nations Environment Programme (UNEP), which defines it as one that results in "improved human well-being and social equity, while significantly reducing environmental risks and ecological scarcities." In its simplest expression, a green economy can be thought of as one which is low carbon, resource efficient and socially inclusive.[177] It also means that the ability to produce the clean energy, which also allows technologies and production processes with the products that consume lesser energy and carbon content. The concept of green economy is also linked to the green growth and natural capital with the interaction of environmental systems. It is one whose growth in income and employment is driven by public and private investments that reduce carbon emissions and pollution, enhance energy and resource efficiency, and prevent the loss of biodiversity and ecosystem services.[178] The Green Economy is one in which the vital linkages among the economy, society and environment are taken into account and in which the transformation of production processes and consumption patterns while contributing to a reduced waste, pollution and the efficient use of resources, materials, and energy. It will revitalize and diversify economies, create decent employment opportunities, promote sustainable trade, reduce poverty, and improve equity and income distribution.[179] In other words, green economy is an environment-friendly approach. Among the most destructive and highly contributory to the climate change is the burning of fossil fuels. Oil-powered cars and vehicles have largely contributed to CO_2 emissions. Thus, electric vehicles will flood streets and highways in the near future because of the commitment of many nations to significant reduction of CO_2 emissions. As China rises, green economy has the best chance. China proclaimed itself as the first Green Superpower. Unfortunately, rare materials used in electric vehicle battery are mined in different countries to the destruction of mountains, forests and damaging the whole ecosystem. Soil erosion, flash floods and landslides are frequent in mining areas and surrounding areas. The sad reality is that development has always been inseparable with disaster.

It is highly significant to take into account that post-industrial society which is characterized by technology and innovation has high contribution to climate change. Climate Change is the outcome of man's handiwork. Its effects and impacts are all-embracing. Furthermore, global warming has an impact on the activities of ice in Arctic region or North Pole. The melting of the ice has been a reality for couple of decades now. Walsh disclosed that coastal communities in Alaska and Siberia are experiencing increased flooding and coastal erosion as a result of the loss of the sea ice buffer that previously protected the coast from wind-driven waves during summer and autumn storms. As a result, several communities in Alaska are facing costly relocation away from the coast. An increase in ship traffic is another impact of the retreating sea ice cover.[180]

The solutions proposed by the western politicians, whether they are solutions from the Kyoto-Conference, the EU's Climate Plan or the UN Climate Conference in Copenhagen (COP15) all confirm the lack of interest in the environment and climate if the western companies have to pay the price.[181] The paramount solution to the climate change is following the injunction of the Holy Quran which commands how to take care of God's creation. The blueprint of capitalism states that any country is free to exercise its will without consideration of the welfare of the global citizen. This is why many Muslim scholars would state that Islam is the solution.

_____

The Future of Islam in Focus

The Middle East or the Muslim world in general is historically heavily shaped by outside powers. Starting from the Sykes-Picot Agreement, the Muslim world was under the oppressive environment. It has just started to shape itself, albeit in a violent and destructive way. The political turmoil in many Middle East countries is exacerbated by the COVID-19. Easing the risks posed by the deep-rooted and volatile conflicts in the face of the pandemic demands thoughtful policy and other actions at the national, regional and global levels, all at the same time.[182] Muslims need to rethink and reshape the Muslim world for the better. Indeed, the Ummah should try to recreate itself and look for its potential to build a better world. Steven and Ross recommended that to avoid the worst outcomes for an already fraught region, there is no substitute and frankly no alternative to some forms of cooperation among regional actors, and ideally international actors as well. With the Middle East likely to emerge from the COVID-19 crisis more fragile and potentially explosive than before, a cooperative architecture that can build regional resilience is imperative. Policymakers should look at some of the scenarios outlined above as both a wakeup call and an opportunity to move toward such architecture.[183]

As reset marches, regional powers will walk in equal footing with US in the table of power. The Muslim world will produce a number of regional powers especially in Middle East. The rivalry between the three kings of Mideast will be intensified: Iran, Saudi Arabia and Turkey. As mentioned previously, these three countries have their respective interests in the Muslim world. During 2011 Arab uprisings, there were three groups of countries in the Middle East conflict: Saudi Arabia, Qatar-Turkey and Iran group; Lebanon-Iraq-Syria group and Jordan-Oman-Israel group. Saudi Arabia, Qatar-Turkey and Iran were the drivers in shaping the regional conflict. They were heads of power contest in Middle East. They could not bear to see one on top holding the hammer of power. Lebanon, Iraq and Syria were sucked into the conflict. The three Kings were immensely involved in the conflicts troubling the three countries. Jordan, Oman and Israel had parochial interest in the regional conflict and that they were primarily focused on security and stability at home. They charted independent paths, though Israel's biggest interest is the weakening of Iran and its resistance axis. Back in 2004, King Abdullah of Jordan was already referring to a threat from an emerging "Shia Crescent of Power" in Mideast. He warned the Sunni countries of this crescent becoming a full moon. The Sunni leaders were alarmed of this growing development and in response mercenaries were trained in Jordan, which later became the pillar of powerful uprisings against Iran-backed Assad.

The Arab revolution changed the political landscape and accelerated geopolitical configuration of the Arab world. ISIS established a short-lived caliphate in Syria and Iraq. The mass uprisings in North Africa which, knocked down the existing powers-that-be, were dissimilar with what happened in Syria. Leaders in North African countries were toppled through mass demonstrations while in Arab Middle East the regional powers mobilized the revolution using the people. In fact, the first country where the Gulf Powers fought against one another was in Syria. The entry of Gulf powers in Syria was easy despite the national borders because they had maintained strong relations with their regional relatives. Intermarriage involving Syrian tribal leaders and Gulf Royals was common. There were occasions that gulf leaders would be invited to solve tribal disputes. Some of the Syrian tribal members who regularly travel to gulf would become naturalized citizens of Qatar and Saudi Arabia. These deep relationships between the Gulf Royals and tribal leaders became an important source of political and economic influence that the Gulf countries have effectively used. The Gulf countries had one important goal in Syria, along with many others, and that was to remove it from Iranian influence employing strategic diplomacy. Saudi Arabia enticed Syria to join its alliance and group. In 2009 and 2010, Assad visited Riyadh at least three times and in return the King of Saudi Arabia also visited Syria. Qatar had also good diplomatic relations with Syria. Eventually, Assad had developed a strong personal and political relationship with the Emir of Qatar and the King of Saudi Arabia. Gulf witnessed and felt that the time was ripe to finally pull Syria into their orbit. However, Iranian grip to Assad was as good as the Gulf Royals. This was unacceptable for the two Gulf countries that Syria had two masters. Afterwards, they worked and supported the opposition's uprisings. In the initial stage of uprising in Syria, Qatar, Turkey and Saudi Arabia had one goal, that is, to remove Syria from Iran's orbit.

While the civil war was raging, Saudi Arabia and Qatar along with Turkey found themselves supporting different groups in the opposition. This accelerated their rift and rivalry. Qatar together with Turkey intended to use the influence of the Muslim Brotherhood to steer the transitional period in Syrian with MB dominated the military and political bodies. Brotherhood-link groups were Liwan al-Tawhid in Aleppo and Ahfad al-Rasul in Idlid. In contrary, Riyadh supported western-allied non-Islamists group of FSA under military supreme command led by General Salim Idris. It also mobilized Salafi-leaning forces of Ahram al-Sham.

To counter the growing uprisings, Iran organized People's Army known as Jaysh al-Shabi consisting regime supporters from Alawites and others with estimated more or less 100,000 member-fighters. The main goal was to prevent Syria to be used against Iran. The Iranian policies were implemented by Iran Revolutionary Guard Corps (IRGC) particularly elite Quds Force headed by the late Gen. Qassem Soleimani. In addition, Iran has been understood as the face of resistance against the US Empire for decades now. It exported its revolution in Mideast starting from Lebanon when it created the Hezbollah. The Iranian revolution was able to spread Iran's influence in several countries including Yemen, Iraq, Syria, Lebanon and Palestine. The persistent resistance of Assad with the support coming from Iran put Qatar and Saudi in disarray. Two important reasons why Qatar softened its ambition in Syria: the removal of its ally in Egypt, Dr. Muhammad Morsi, by a coup and the loss of its favored commanders in Syrian opposition. Though Qatar was an ally of Turkey, what prevented it to massively support the opposition was its concern over the status of Syrian Kurds. Turkey focused on limiting the potential of Syrian Kurds to secure autonomy as it would possibly become a launch pad of military support to the PKK, which is the archenemy of the Republic of Turkey.

Saudi Arabia and Iran have both been deeply involved in the Syrian civil war from its beginning in 2011, each sponsoring rival sides. Both have utilized sectarian identity politics to further their goals and both have contributed to the growth of violence along sectarian lines. This has led to a categorization by many that both are sectarian actors that immediately reach for identity politics as a tool of influence. However, a closer examination of the Syrian case would challenge this perception and it can be argued that in Syria, identity politics was not the immediate policy pursued by either Saudi Arabia or Iran.[184] The main reason of Riyadh-Tehran conflict is control and power. When they could not achieve their goal, they use sectarian card to further embitter the situation for their political objectives. This is so obvious in Syria when tension was interpreted as sectarian one, which is a pure lie. In Bahrain, sectarian card was also used. In Syria, minority Alawi sect controls the government while majority Sunni population lives in poverty. In contrary, Bahrain is Shia-majority country with Sunni elite controls the government. In other words, the Plan B of Saudi Arabia and Iran to advance their respective interest in the region is to use the sectarian card.

Another country devastated by civil war is Libya after the fall of Muammar Qaddafi in 2011. Britain armed East Libya and marched to Tripoli. Militias supported by Britain dominated Libyan powerful city. NATO-led occupation of Libya had successfully dislodged Qaddafi from position of power. After the fall of the strongman of North Africa, Britain and France created political leadership called National Transition Council (NTC) in February 2011. NTC would serve as the political face of the revolution and that 100 countries recognized it as the sole representative of Libyan government. Ironically, the NTC leadership was mainly composed of people from the former Qaddafi regime such as Mahmud Jibril, who was formerly a head of economic department. In 2012, permanent government was established General National Congress (GNC) with Mahmud Jibril as its head. In June 25, 2014, America hurried the emergence of the former General Khalifa Haftar and afterwards attacked Tripoli and the parliament. Looking back, General Haftar was responsible for the toppling of King Idris. He was captured in Chad and disowned by Qaddafi in 1986. Later, CIA negotiated his release and subsequently spent next 20 years in Virginia. His homecoming was assisted by US and even Russia. The forces of Gen. Haftar were maintained by western powers, Egypt and UAE.

Following the dissolution of the GNC, two competing governments in Libya emerged: the Government of National Accord (GNA) and the Haftar-led government. The government of warlord Gen. Haftar was supported by many countries as mentioned above such as UAE, Egypt, United States, Russia and other European powers. Libya during Qaddafi, which was an envy of many governments in the world, collapsed. Presently, Libya became an arena of competition between Abu Dhabi and Doha along with Ankara. Abu Dhabi supplied Gen. Haftar with powerful weapons when his forces attacked Tripoli. In opposing group, Ankara supported the government in Tripoli against Gen. Haftar.

Iraq is also a theater of conflict among the Three Kings with different interests at clash. Iran stepped in Iraq after US departure when it was devastated by war. Iraq was at terrible war with ISIS. Gen. Soleimani was commissioned to clear Iraq of ISIS, which patently destroyed the balance in Mideast. Iran groomed the post-American Iraq. It had thousands of militias at work and it also entered Iraqi politics. Iran was so assertive than its rival. Saudi Arabia was particular with the stability of Iraq without Iran. Turkey wanted status quo in Kurdistan, Iraq, fearing that a more powerful Kurdistan might support the PKK.

Iraq has been a playhouse of Tehran-Riyadh regional rivalry. Tehran has been significantly more active in attempting to gain influence in Iraq than Riyadh has since 2003. This is because it was especially alarmed by the sudden rise of U.S. military power and influence in its neighboring states of Iraq and Afghanistan. This rise of U.S. influence and involvement in both Iraq and Afghanistan occurred shortly after President George W. Bush had identified Iran as part of "an axis of evil." Such rhetoric contributed to the Iranian view that they were now being encircled by enemies led by a particularly hostile power.[185]

This Iranian effort has involved diplomacy, economic investment, covert action and cultivating Iranian patrons within the Iraqi political system including the leadership of armed Shia militias. This approach has produced results, and Iran has emerged as a major power in domestic Iraqi politics. Iraq's former Prime Minister Maliki, who was drawing on a Shi'ite domestic power base, was reluctant to offend Tehran, and had stated that strategic ties between the two nations served the interest of both.[186] In theological line, majority of Iraqi populations are Shias. In fact, Ayatollah Sistani, the most prominent Shia religious scholar is living in Iraq. He was able to mobilize Iraqi citizens to exercise democratic procedure in post-American Iraq. He is respected in the Shia world and even in Sunni Iraqis.

Another area of conflict was in Yemen. Yemen suffered from worst humanitarian crisis. Iran and Saudi supported the two opposing camps. Houthis are trained, funded, mobilized, and operated by Tehran. They occasionally threw numerous missiles in Saudi Arabia and they could be foiled by the avant-garde air defense system. In response, Saudi had to drop bombs in Yemen. Turkey's role was purely on humanitarian aspect. As seen in the foregoing, the division of Ummah is an indispensable obstacle in creating a stronger Islam. Mideast countries would fight one another so brutal and inhumane, ignoring the basic principle of brotherhood in Islam. Yemen has experienced the most disheartening and miserable situation in the world. Yemenis are pounded by the rivalry of the two Muslim powers.

The Three Kings have variegated positions in different countries. Turkey is determined to revive the Ottoman Empire. It shows its military, economic, political and cultural potential to restore the lost glory of Ottomans. It is involved politically and militarily in countries which were former Ottoman territories. Turkey does not care if neo-Ottoman project is realized through its independent power or through NATO support. Ironically, NATO could not allow a caliphate system returning in world politics. Iranian revolution is confined and focused only in Middle East. It has no interest in dipping its hand in North African politics. Unlike Turkey, UAE, Qatar and Saudi Arabia with overstretching powers as they influenced many political situations in Africa and central Asia.

The Three Kings have different approaches to Israel. Iran and Saudi Arabia have no diplomatic ties with the Zionist state. Turkey has diplomatic relations with Israel. Present King of Saudi has a bitter experience with Israel. He witnessed King Faisal's defiance against US and Israel. This conflict of interest among the three kings give Israel a chance and opportunity to empower itself while they are busy pitting against one another. Presently, the Arab world – at least the established governments, with the exception of Saudi Arabia – has been in friendship and alliance with Israel. UAE, Bahrain, Egypt, Sudan, Morocco and others have recognized Israel. The other Arab countries are soaked in an endless instability such as Iraq, Syria, Lebanon, Yemen and Libya among others. Therefore, presently, there are two types of Arab countries: Israel's friends and allies and the battered Arab countries.

Israel's friends and allies are at on-call for Israel while the battered Arab countries are weak enough and that they are busy in their respective recovery and rehabilitation initiatives. Lebanon for instance is in deep crisis. Political and economic crises in Lebanon are raging on. The perceived short-term solution is to borrow money in the IMF and WB for economic and political recovery. The miserable economic situation in Lebanon exacerbated political crisis. This move is not without consequence. Before the crisis, Lebanon is a home of resistance but now there is no recovery in sight. Hezbollah is also deeply affected – its military power and manpower. Lebanon will be pressured by leaders to recognize Israel even Hezbollah detests it. The situation in Middle East is a perfect timing for Israel to hold Arab world's neck.

Understanding the rivalry between Saudi Arabia and Iran goes some way in understanding the uncertainty and instability that play out across the contemporary Middle East. There is little doubt that the rivalry has shaped regional politics in a number of ways, contingent upon political and socio-economic contexts and agenda of Riyadh and Tehran. Although the rivalry occupies a central role in the construction of regional security, it is overly simplistic to reduce Middle Eastern politics solely to a bi-polar struggle between Saudi Arabia and Iran with a number of additional actors adding to the complexity of regional politics. Indeed, the role of the UAE, Israel, Turkey, Qatar, and others cannot be ignored, as these issues exacerbate an increasingly troubled situation.[187]

In COVID-19 period, there are four country-factions in the Islamic world particularly in Middle East: Saudi-led coalition, Axis of Resistance, Political Islamist and Jihadi Islamist. First, Saudi-led coalition was organized during the war in Yemen. The coalition is mainly composed of Saudi Arabia, UAE, Egypt and Bahrain. There were also others which joined the invasion. The alliance installed its pawn in battle-scarred Yemen. Saudi-led coalition imposed Qatar blockade; this was then a saber-rattling scenario. Second, the political Islamist faction is Turkey-Qatar-Muslim Brotherhood alliance. When Muslim Brothers were defeated in Egypt, Qatar opened its door for them. Muslim brothers were scattered in Mideast far and wide. Before the Arab revolution, they were able to penetrate governments through political parties, as they joined politics. They had influences in Jordan, Morocco and Tunisia. Political Islam as an ideology of the Brothers found its way to Turkey and Qatar. In 2021, Qatar held a first parliamentary election giving rise to a sort of Qatari democracy. The members of the parliament who were previously appointed personalities suddenly became elected. Political Islamist ideology advanced the idea of joining the secular system; but it would introduce reform on it. Political Islamists could thrive in a secular system without compromising Islamic values. Obviously, Turkey-Qatar axis does not want to destroy the system of nation-states but rather it uses democracy to improve the situation of the Ummah.

The third faction is the Iran-led axis of resistance, shaking the regional order. As previously mentioned, the axis of resistance is composed of Iran, Houthis in Yemen, Hezbollah in Lebanon, Assad-led Syrian government and the Hamas in Palestine. Iran's main objective is to liquidate the Zionist State and the western allies in Middle East specifically Saudi Arabia. For Iran, recognition of the state of Israel is a betrayal to the Palestinian cause. Despite numerous economic woes, Iran was able to survive decades of US sanctions. It operated the situation in Iraq and Syria to the defeat of ISIS.

The fourth faction, Jihadi Islamist, still exists in the Muslim world. Jihadi Islamists are non-state actors with high concentration in Iraq-Syria, Somalia, Afghanistan-Pakistan, South East Asia and the Sahel region in Africa. The mission of this group is to facilitate the return of the ideal Salafi system in the Islamic world disregarding the modern development that humanity is in. The biggest militant movements advancing Jihadi Islamist ideology are Al-Qaeda and the ISIS. Subsequent to the death of Osama Bin Laden, Al-Qaeda remained weak and disorganized. It was then revived in Syria in the form of Al-Nusra Front fighting the Assad regime. There is no central command following its defeat in Syria. Moreover, ISIS was defeated by joint cooperation of the world and regional powers in Middle East. The caliphate system they spread was dismantled and remained inoperative. ISIS like Al-Qaeda, there is no central command directing a well-coordinated move.

Though before the COVID-19 setting, the Muslim world particularly Middle East was in chaos. Two decades before the onset of COVID-19, the Muslim world has experienced at least three powerful political earthquakes that result to new geopolitical alignment. The first overwhelming shake was in 2001. The Muslim world was attacked by America as retaliation to Twin Tower attack. The ensuing chaos brought about by the US attack in Middle East particularly Iraq and Afghanistan put the Ummah in a sorry situation. The NATO and the whole US allies responded to America's war on terror. Muslims around the world were affected emotionally, socially and even economically. The strongman of Iraq Saddam Hussein and the Taliban-led Afghan government suffered crushing defeats from the US-led coalition. Governments against the US were removed from the power and then US installed puppet regimes. War on Terror effectively removed threats against imperial rule.

The second devastating shake was in 2011. The dictators of Tunisia, Libya, Yemen and Egypt fell. People of North Africa and the Mideast were gleefully celebrating their victory until the western world intervened and clandestinely injected their interests hijacking the people's revolution. This revolution was called, "Arab Spring." Before Arab Spring, President Hosni Mubarak of Egypt had no better relations with Iran and Saudi Arabia. The two kings had an interest to see Hosni Mubarak ousted in Egypt. Consequently, Iran openly supported the revolution. While the uprising was still in progress, Saudi Arabia seeing the revolution with brotherhood's color, remained silent and actively waited for the results. Turkey, Qatar and Iran were in one page during the revolution. The victory of the revolution facilitated the rise of Dr. Morsi to power in Egypt. Dr. Morsi was congratulated by Iranian government and then Iran-Egypt diplomatic relations were stamped. The emergence of Dr. Morsi was not favorable to Saudi Arabia-UAE axis; this led to a coup staged by military under AbdulFatah Al-Sisi's command. UAE and Saudi bankrolled the successful military coup in Egypt. Later, Al-Sisi initiated several reforms and through this Egypt became a bridge to UAE in manipulating the situation in Libya. The ultimate outcome of the second shake is the successful removal of former western puppets. And then western countries were able to put another set of leaders in the Muslim world. After a decade, the leaders of the Muslim world who were no longer useful to American masters faced powerful uprisings from their own people. The three Kings became more aggressive to such an extent that they openly deploy their state forces to assist their allies. Turkey sent forces to Libya, Syria, Iraq and Azerbaijan with an aim of showing the world of its potential to be a world power. Saudi Arabia invaded Yemen to fight the Houthis. The war in Yemen is one of the dirtiest wars that have ever occurred in all world history. Iran mobilized an army in various Mideast countries including, Iraq and Syria. The third shake occurred in 2020, by far the most powerful, that is, the recognition of the Arab states to the state of Israel. Abraham Accords are sets of agreements between the Israel and the four Arab States namely: Bahrain, UAE, Sudan and Morocco. The recognition of Israel by Arab States is not just for the sake of establishing diplomatic relations. It has huge implication in the future relations of Arab States and Iran. The legitimacy and acceptability of Israel to its Arab neighbors are significantly bolstered. The Muslim world is evidently trekking more difficult journey in the future. The conflict among the three kings and their allies are increasingly deepened, that means, Riyadh-Tehran geopolitical fissure will stay for years with no sign of reconciliation. Expectedly, a Riyadh-Tel-Aviv alliance countering Iran's expansion will be forged in the near future. Saudi has been indirectly and covertly cooperating with Israel since the rise of Muhammad Bin Salman. The establishment of diplomatic relations between the two countries is expected sooner than later. Iran is openly supporting and funding Hamas (of Palestine) which is the archenemy of Israel. So, the two countries have common interest, and that is, removing Iranian grip in the region. It can be argued that Israel has all the reasons to simultaneously attack Damascus, Hezbollah and Hamas after it will secure the go-signal of Saudi Arabia and that will happen after forging their official diplomatic relations. The administration of United States of America is still pursuing the project of erstwhile US President, Donald Trump, of mediating the Arab states and Israeli friendship and alliance. The official relations between Israel and Saudi Arabia can be inked anytime as they even greatly overlapped the interests of US in the Middle East. US would just be happy seeing Iran contained but Israel and Saudi Arabia want Iran defeated militarily and politically. The present situation in the Arab world indicates a turbulent future. The disunity will further embitter the already bitter situation. Israel will be able to use this disunity for its advantage. Qatar and Oman had undeclared recognition of Israel, though they did not openly admit it.

Multiple countries in the region, including Qatar, Bahrain and Oman established connections with Israel in the 1990s after the Palestine Liberation Organization (PLO) and Israel signed the Oslo Accords.[188] Saudi Arabia, as part of this axis of like-minded states pursuing coordinated foreign policy objectives, shares strategic motivations with the UAE and Bahrain in regard to Israel. Indeed, Riyadh and Tel Aviv have cooperated covertly for years, mostly around security issues and intelligence-sharing, but the Gulf kingdom has its own calculus in terms of its readiness to formalize relations. The covert cooperation of Saudi and Israel is primarily engendered by the continuing rise of Iran. They have strategic interests, while Iranian revolution is facing problems brought about by the Lebanese crisis and the longstanding US-imposed sanction of Iran.[189]

Saudi Arabia cannot openly embrace Israel because it will have a devastating effect on Ummah. This includes its unique status in the Islamic world as the custodian of the two holiest places in Islam, and the legitimacy the House of Saud must protect in that role. The country is also much larger and more diverse than its counterparts, with powerful segments that do not perceive Israel favorably.[190] Many religious leaders do not want Israeli-Saudi friendship especially the Salafis who constitute the mainstream population. The power of Saudi Arabia is stemming from the religious scholars who propagate its values around the world. It has a unique locus in the heart of Ummah given its irrefutable status as a birthplace of Islam, and by embracing Israel, which is seen as oppressor of Palestine, will destroy its credibility as a center and guardian of Islam.

Furthermore, contrary to the historically normative view of Israel in the Arab world, the UAE holds Israel to be neither an enemy nor threat to regional stability. According to the worldview of Abu Dhabi's Crown Prince Sheikh Mohammed bin Zayed Al Nahyan, who has been the de facto leader of the emirate since his elder brother's stroke in 2014, the principal threats to the UAE and its allies are an expansionist Iran and transnational political Islamists.[191]

Political Islamist is the Turkey-Qatar Axis, yet the divide still persists in the Gulf due to political tug-of-war between Turkey-Qatar axis and Saudi-UAE bloc. Since a couple of decades ago, sectarian card was used to play around Middle East politics – as Iranian expansionism and ISIS Caliphate dominated the regional order – but the future will be slightly different and that Sunni countries will be at each other's face, though, Riyadh-Tehran rivalry will still stay for some time. The dream of Turkish Ottoman revival is a direct threat to Saudi Arabia and UAE. Having the Saudi-UAE axis caught between the Iranian expansionist and interventionist policies and Turkish super state dream, it will come to Israel's door for help.

Another important development in the Islamic world is the reemergence of Taliban in Afghanistan. Former Taliban government's relationship with Saudi Arabia was characterized by mutual trust while Taliban-Iran relationship was full of hatred, ill will and animosity. After 20 years, Taliban is back. Saudi Arabia immediately sent a message of friendship in post-Taliban takeover while the rest of Ummah is still waiting for its political posture in relation to Israel. It is with basic analysis that one can conclude that Taliban has learned their lessons the hard way from their tempestuous history. Aggressiveness and brutality were removed from their lexicons. Surprisingly, before the takeover, Taliban had diplomatic visits to Iran, China and Russia. Iran has been vocal in supporting the cause of the Taliban against the dying superpower.

There are two possible steps that Taliban would employ in relation to Middle East's power-struggle. It will either show open rejection to Arab-Israeli friendship or remain neutral in the face of competing Arab-Persian Powers. Taliban-led Afghanistan and Iran will be friends – in the sense that they will not mess each other – but not allies. Alliance in political vocabulary is deeper than friendship. Allies will come to each other's rescue to defeat the enemy. In the case of Israeli-Arab and Iran war, Taliban will not dip its hand.

To sum it up, the future regional order will be characterized by rivalry between Iran and Israel on the one hand and Turkey-Saudi on the other. Pakistan and Afghanistan may revive the Mogul empire to such an extent that their relationship will even become closer. Many analysts opined that the defeat of US in Afghanistan will herald a new beginning. There is an unbelievable attachment between the elite group in Pakistan and the Taliban. Moreover, Sunni-majority countries such as Pakistan and Afghanistan will neither openly side with Iran nor support Israel. The Sunni Arab states, which orbit on Saudi-UAE axis, will definitely turn out to be anti-Iran forces.

In the long run, a political estimate highlights an assumption of the rise of authoritarian leaders in the Arab world. In post-pandemic era, the two crown princes of Saudi Arabia and UAE will surely occupy the seat of power; MBS and MBZ are the de facto leaders of the two powerful countries in the Arab World. They are pro-Israel hands down. The next Arab leaders will have great responsibility in remaking or unmaking the current regional order. Saudi Arabia and UAE are oil-rich countries which would feel the agonizing effects of the rise of electric vehicles. The demands of oil will fall sharply. UAE will suffer fatal economic crisis, so will Saudi Arabia.

Yes, the driving force behind UAE and specifically Dubai's growth has been largely its oil wealth, followed by companies that are run by foreign workers. Its position as a trading hub has also brought it wealth. The problem with this is that the oil is not unlimited, and is already running out. The skilled workers that are helping to develop the service sector are mostly from overseas, with only a tiny part of Dubai's population now considered to be native Arabs. These reasons show why Dubai is nothing more than a mirage in the desert. Its growth and survival are dependent upon the talent and expertise of foreign entities. It can only offer specialist services such as banking and finance as a means to guarantee its future, along with tourism. As these sectors rely heavily on the goodwill and confidence of foreigners, Dubai is vulnerable to economic collapse if ever these powers decide to pull out.[192]

Similarly, Riyadh is dependent to its oil revenues. The collapse of Saudi and UAE is an important turning point in Middle East history as Israel will take advantage of the situation to finally hold the Arab world, while the Riyadh-Abu Dhabi bloc will approach Israel begging for help. Israel will at last appear powerful and mighty holding the axe. The vision 2030 of MBS will not be sustainable as there is no potential alternative to oil revenues. Tourism and Hajj revenues cannot be comparable with the profits the oil can give.

With all this mind-bending cracks, the world is waiting for an alternative ideology that will put an end to global conflict and misery. Similar with other groups of people, the Muslim world has been waiting for Masihi ideological paradigm. What is Masihi paradigm? Masihi paradigm is an essential form of overarching system derived from the Holy Scriptures. Masih is an epithet of Prophet Isa (AS). It is stated in the Holy Quran that the 'sign of all signs' of the final hour is the reappearance of Prophet Isa (AS) in the center-stage of global affairs. Upon his arrival, he will witness a ruling Israel. The ruling elite, who plotted to kill him in Jerusalem two thousand years ago, will rule again in his reappearance.

Prophet Isa was born into an Israelite community, and hence belonged to a people who claimed, and still claim to this day, that they are a special people with the Lord-God who chose them from amongst all of mankind and conferred upon them a special status with Himself. They were expecting a Messiah who was promised to them by the Lord-God, and who when he came, would restore the golden age when Jews ruled the world.[193] This is why, in the end of time, after two millennia, the state of affairs will return. Jews had persecuted him two thousand years ago and in the mysterious turn of history, Jews will come to power for the final judgment to fulfill the apocalyptic battle between the forces of Dajjal and Masih. In the end, Prophet Isa (AS) will appear victorious then Masihi international order will begin.

Endnotes

Part One

The Rise of Islam

1. See the book of Ibn Khaldun (1969). N.J. Dawood (ed.). The Muqaddima published in Princeton University Press.
2. Samuel Huntington (1927–2008) was an American political scientist, adviser, and academic. He spent more than half a century at Harvard University where he was director of Harvard's Center for International Affairs.
3. Fukuyama is known for his book The End of History and the Last Man (1992), which argues that the worldwide spread of liberal democracies and free-market capitalism of the west and its lifestyle may signal the end point of humanity's sociocultural evolution and become the final form of human government. However, his subsequent book *Trust: Social Virtues and Creation of Prosperity* (1995) modified his earlier position to acknowledge that culture cannot be cleanly separated from economics. Fukuyama is also associated with the rise of the neoconservative movement from which he has since distanced himself.
4. Former President of Islamic Republic of Iran, for his endorsement of and continuous campaign for a constructive civilizational dialogue paradigm, as an ideal rule of the game in the relations among nations, see Khatami's address before UNESCO General Conference

on October 29, 1999, "Discourse: An Iranian Quarterly 1, no. 2 (Fall 1999): 208-216.
5. Bilgrin's book on Civilization, Dialogue, Security: The Challenge Of Post-Secularism And The Limits Of Civilizational Dialogue, published British International Studies Association
6. i.e. excommunicating other Muslims as outside the pale of Islam
7. The Taliban which refers to itself as the Islamic Emirate of Afghanistan is a Deobandi Islamic Fundamentalist political movement and military organization in Afghanistan. The Taliban's ideology has been described as combining an "innovative" form of Sharia Islamic law based on Deobandi fundamentalism and militant Islamism, combined with Pashtun social and cultural norms known as Pashtunwali as most Taliban are Pashtun tribesmen.
8. Al-Qaeda is a militant movement organized by Osama Bin Laden which masterminded many attacks against the western countries. It is the primary suspect of the 9/11 Twin Tower attack.
9. Boko-Haram is a militant organization based in Africa specifically in Nigeria which prohibited western education.
10. Al-Shabab is an Al-Qaeda-link militant movement operating in Somalia and other neighboring countries.
11. Islamic State of Iraq and Syria is a global terrorist organization which seeks for the return of the ideal world of the righteous predecessors. It wants to establish a

global caliphate governed by strict Sharia based on ISIS's interpretations.
12. Surat an-Nahl, 125
13. Schwartz, 2003, Two Faces of Islam
14. Ibid
15. Suratul Ma'ida 5: Verse 51.
16. Ottoman Empire, empire created by Turkish tribes in Anatolia (Asia Minor) that grew to be one of the most powerful states in the world during the 15th and 16th centuries. The Ottoman period spanned more than 600 years and came to an end only in 1922, when it was replaced by the Turkish Republic and various successor states in southeastern Europe and the Middle East. At its height the empire encompassed most of southeastern Europe to the gates of Vienna, including present-day Hungary, the Balkan region, Greece, and parts of Ukraine; portions of the Middle East now occupied by Iraq, Syria, Israel and Egypt; North Africa as far west as Algeria; and large parts of the Arabian Peninsula.
17. Arab Spain was governed by Islam for centuries and that it was a continuation of Umayyad Caliphate after it was toppled by Abbasids.
18. The Abbasid Caliphate was the third caliphate to succeed the Islamic government established by prophet Muhammad. It was founded by a dynasty descended from Muhammad's Uncle, Abbas ibn Abdul Mutattalib (566–653 CE), from whom the dynasty takes its name. They ruled as caliphs for most of the caliphate from their capital in Bagdad in modern-day Iraq, after

having overthrown the Ummayad Caliphate in the Abbasid Revolution of 750 CE (132 AH).

19. Seljuk is Turkic tribe that invaded southwestern Asia in the 11th century and eventually founded an empire that included Mesopotamia, Syria, Palestine, and most of Iran. Their advance marked the beginning of Turkish power in the Middle East.
20. The North Atlantic Treaty Organization, also called the North Atlantic Alliance, is an intergovernmental military alliance between 28 European countries and 2 North American countries. The organization implements the North Atlantic Treaty that was signed on 4 April 1949.
21. Capitalism is an economic system based on the private ownership of the means of production and their operation for profit. Central characteristics of capitalism include capital accumulation, competitive markets, a price system, private property and the recognition of property rights, voluntary exchange and wage labor.
22. See Morgenthau (2006), p. 66
23. Ahmad Amin, Zuhr Al-Islam 1:18 cited by Mahdi Pishva'i
24. Ibn Kathir, al-Bidayah wa'l-Nihayah 3:144 cited by Mahdi Pishva'i
25. Armstrong, 2002, Islam: A short History. New York: the Modern Library.

26. The Mogul or Moghul Empire was an early modern empire in South Asia. For some two centuries,

the empire stretched from the outer fringes of the Indus basin in the west, northern Afghanistan in the northwest, and Kashmir in the north, to the highlands of present-day Assam and Bangladesh in the east, and the uplands of the Deccan Plateau in South India.

27. Safavid Empire, (1501–1736), was ruled by Safavid dynasty of Iran whose establishment of Twelver Shi'ism as the state religion of Iran was a major factor in the emergence of a unified national consciousness among the various ethnic and linguistic elements of the country.

28. Morgenthau, 2006, Politics among Nations published in New York: McGraw-Hill.

29. Curtis, M. (2008).The Great Political Theories, Vol. 2, New York: Harperperrenial Publishers

30. Musa Kamidon Damao (2021). The Evolutionary Responsefor Bangsamoro Self-Rule. *International Journal of Arts, Humanities and Social Studies*, 3(5), 01-08.

31. Damao, M. (2015). The Comprehensive Agreement on the Bangsamoro: A Stakeholders' Analysis. Cotabato City: Notre Dame Press.

Part Two

The Euro-Centric World Order

32. Middle Ages, the period in European history from the collapse of Roman civilization in the 5th century CE to the period of the Renaissance (variously interpreted as

beginning in the 13th, 14th, or 15th century, depending on the region of Europe and other factors).

33. The French Revolution was a period of radical political and societal change in France that began with the Estates General of 1789 and ended with the formation of the French Consulate in November 1799. Many of its ideas are considered fundamental principles of liberal democracy.

34. Harun al-Rashid was the fifth Abbasid Caliph. His birth date is debated, with various sources giving dates from 763 to 766. His epithet "al-Rashid" translates to "the Orthodox", "the Just", "the Upright", or "the Rightly-Guided". He ruled from 786 to 809, traditionally regarded to be the beginning of the Islamic Golden Age.

35. Lari, M. (2006).Western Civilization Through Muslim Eyes published by Foundation of Islamic Cultural Propagation

36. Fatimid, political and religious dynasty that dominated an empire in North Africa and subsequently in the Middle East from 909 to 1171 CE and tried unsuccessfully to oust the Abbasid caliphs as leaders of the Islamic world. It took its name from Fatima, daughter of the Prophet Muhammad, from whom the Fatimids claimed descent.

37. Keddie, Sayyid Jamal Ad-Din Al-Afghani, p. 133

38. Book of Karabell, Z. entitled, People of the Book: The Forgotten History of Islam and the West, Published by John Murray, London United Kingdom.

39. Al Saud is an Arab clan living in Najd which masterminded rebellion against the Ottoman Empire.

40. Hussein bin Ali Al-Hashimi was an Arab leader from the Banu Hashim clan who was the Sharif Emir of Makkah from 1908 and, after proclaiming the Great Arab Revolt against the Ottoman Empire, King of the Hijaz from 1916 to 1924. At the end of his reign he also briefly laid claim to the office of Caliph. He was a 37th-generation direct descendant of Prophet Muhammad, as he belongs to the Hashemite family.

41. Col. Thomas Edward Lawrence (16 August 1888 – 19 May 1935) was a British archeologist, army officer, diplomat and writer, who became renowned for his role in the Arab Revolt (1916–1918) and the Sinai and Palestine Campaign (1915–1918) against the Ottoman Empire during the WWI. The breadth and variety of his activities and associations, and his ability to describe them vividly in writing, earned him international fame as Lawrence of Arabia, a title used for the 1962 film based on his wartime activities.

42. See Muhammadi, M. (2006). Islamic Revolution and the World System: Imam Khomeini and the International System, IRI: International affairs Department.

43. The term used to refer to a right-wing conspiracy theory that became popular among anti-government extremists from the 1990s onwards. "New World Order" conspiracists believe that a tyrannical, socialist "one-world" conspiracy has already taken over most of the planet and schemes to eliminate the last bastion of

freedom, the United States, with the help of collaborators within the government. Through repressive measures, as well as manufactured crises such as terrorist attacks and pandemics, the globalist conspirators seek to eliminate dissent and to disarm Americans so that the "New World Order" can move in and enslave them.

44. Muhammadi, M. (2006). Islamic Revolution and the World System: Imam Khomeini and the International System, IRI: International affairs Department.

45. GLOBALIZATION is the word used to describe the growing interdependence of the world's economies, cultures, and populations, brought about by cross-border trade in goods and services, technology, and flows of investment, people, and information. Countries have built economic partnerships to facilitate these movements over many centuries.

46. Brown, S. (1991). *Explaining the Transformation of World Politics,* International Journal 46, No. 2, pp. 207-219

47. Betts, R. (2010a). *Conflict or Cooperation: Three Visions Revisited*, United States: Columbia University

48. Betts, R. (2010b). *Conflict or Cooperation: Three Visions Revisited*, United States: Columbia University.

49. Ikenberry J., Mastanduno, M. & Wohlforth, W. (2009). *Introduction Unipolarity, State Behavior, and Systemic Consequences, World Politics,* Volume 61, Number 1,

January 2009, pp. 1-27 (Article), Cambridge University Press

50. Kenneth Waltz, *Theory of International Politics* (Reading, Mass.: Addison-Wesley 1979), 131.

51. See Jannace, W. & Tiffany, P. (2019). *A New World Order: The Rule of Law, or the Law of Rulers?* Fordham International Law Journal, Volume 42, Issue 5 2019 Article 2

52. James, 2006, p. 1

53. Cox, M. (2003) 'The Empire's Back in Town: Or America's Imperial Temptation – Again', *Millennium*, 32 (1), 1–27

54. Abraham Lincoln, annual message to Congress, December 1, 1862 (**http://showcase.netins.net/web/creative/lincoln/speeches/congress.htm**)

55. See Ikenberry J., Mastanduno, M. & Wohlforth, W. (2009). *Introduction Unipolarity, State Behavior, and Systemic Consequences, World Politics,* Volume 61, Number 1, January 2009, pp. 1-27 (Article), Cambridge University Press

56. Ikenberry, J. (2005). *Power and liberal order: America's postwar world order in transition, International Relations of the Asia-Pacific* Volume 5 (2005) 133–152, available at
doi:10.1093/irap/lci112, 017

57. Wohlforth, W. (1999). *The Stability of a Unipolar World, The MIT Press Journals, International Security,* Vol. 24, No. 1, pp. 5-41
   http://mitpress.mit.edu/journals
58. Zala, B. (2013). *Rethinking Polarity for the Twenty-first Century:*
   Perceptions of Order in International Society, University of Birmingham

59. On January 16, 1991, President George H. W. Bush announced the start of what would be called Operation Desert Storm—a military operation to expel occupying Iraqi forces from Kuwait, which Iraq had invaded and annexed months earlier. For weeks, a U.S.-led coalition of two dozen nations had positioned more than 900,000 troops in the region, most stationed on the Saudi-Iraq border. A U.N.-declared deadline for withdrawal passed on January 15, with no action from Iraq, so coalition forces began a five-week bombardment of Iraqi command and control targets from air and sea.

60. The Korean War was a war fought between North Korea and South Korea from 25 June 1950 to 27 July 1953. The war began on 25 June 1950 when North Korea invaded South Korea following clashes along the border and insurrections in the south. North Korea had military support from the People's Republic of China and the Soviet Russia while South Korea was supported by the UN, principally the US. The fighting ended with an armistice on 27 July 1953

61. The Vietnam War also known as the American War in Vietnam and the Second Indochina War was a conflict in Vietnam, Laos and Cambodia from 1 November 1955 to the fall of Saigon on 30 April 1975. It was the second of the Indochina Wars and was officially fought between North Vietnam and South Vietnam. North Vietnam was supported by the Soviet Union, China and other communist allies; South Vietnam was supported by the US, South Korea, Philippines, Australia, Thailand and other anti-communist allies. The war, considered a Cold War-proxy by some, lasted almost 20 years, with direct U.S. involvement ending in 1973, and included the Laotian and the Cambodian Civil War, which ended with all three countries becoming communist states in 1975.

62. Khan, Adnan (2021) *Strategic Estimate 2021*, available at **www.khilafah.com**

Part Three

The Symptoms of the Sick Empire

63. Porter, P. (2013). Sharing Power? Prospects for A U.S. Concert-Balance Strategy, US: Strategic Studies Institute.

64. Krastev, I. & Leonard, M. (2021).*The Crisis of American Power: How Europeans See Biden's America,* European Council on Foreign Relations

65. Quinn, A. & Kitchen, N (2019) *Understanding American Power: Conceptual Clarity, Strategic Priorities, and the Decline Debate*, Vol. 10, Issue1, US: Global Policy Durham University and John Wiley & Sons Ltd.
66. Boers refer to the descendants of the proto-Afrikaans-speaking Free Burghers of the Eastern Cape frontier in Southern Africa during the 17th, 18th, and 19th centuries. From 1652 to 1795, the Dutch East India Company controlled this area, but the UK incorporated it into the British Empire in 1806 The name of the group is derived from "boer," which means "farmer" in Dutch and Afrikaans.
67. Zakaria, 2008
68. Zakaria, F. (2008). *The Future of American Power How America Can Survive the Rise of the Rest,* US: From Foreign Affairs, Council on Foreign Relations
69. Paul Kennedy. *The Rise and Fall of the Great Powers: Economic Change and Military Conflict from 1500 to 2000* (Random House,1987). The classic argument that global military dominance leads to economic decline.
70. Ashford, E. (2020). *The Aftermath: American Power after COVID-19.* Rome, Italy, Istituto Affari Internazionali (IAI)
71. www.hizb-ut-tahrir.org (Analysis on the Decline in the Political Influence of the United States and its Aftermath)
72. Third Rome refers to the doctrine that Russia or, specifically, Moscow succeeded Rome and

Byzantium Rome as the ultimate center of true Christianity and of the Roman Empire. This is expression of Russia's new place in the world resulting from domestic and international events of the 1430s and 1520s. The monk Filofei of the Pskov-Eliazarov monastery formulated it in one or two epistles, written between 1523 and 1526, which were then reworked during the sixteenth and seventeenth centuries.

73. Third Temple is a structure to be built in Jerusalem which is a long term plan of the State of Israel. The first Temple was constructed by King Solomon (Nabi Sulaiman) and the second was reconstructed in post-Babylonian captivity until it was razed to the ground by Roman Empire.

74. Recep Tayyip Erdoğan is a Turkish politician serving as the current President of Turkey since 2014. He previously served as PM of Turkey from 2003 to 2014 and as Mayor of Istanbul from 1994 to 1998. He founded the Justice and Development Party (AKP) in 2001, leading it to election victories in 2002, 2007 and 2011 before being required to stand down upon his election as president in 2014. He later returned to the AKP leadership in 2017 following the constitutional referendum that year. Coming from an Islamist political background and self-describing as a conservative democrat, he has promoted socially conservative and populist policies during his administration

75. Feffer, J. 2010. Forget China: Turkey is the Next Superpower, available at:

https://www.salon.com/2010/06/14/turkey_rising_superpower/

76. Ibid
77. Entessar, N. (1992). Kurdish Ethnonationalism, London: Lynne Rienner Publishers.
78. Morgenthau, H. (2006). *Politics Among Nations.* New York: McGraw-Hill.
79. Ibid
80. See Islamic Threat: Myth or Reality by John Esposito.
81. Shah System is a system based on the ideas of the former leaders of Iran which was pro-western and secular system. It was toppled was Imam Khomeini revolution.
82. Communism is a philosophical, social, political, and economic ideology and movement whose goal is the establishment of a communist society, namely a socioeconomic order structured upon the ideas of common ownership of the means of production and the absence of social classes, money, and the state.
83. Article 2 of UN Charter p. 629 , Appendix B of Politics Among Nations by Hans Morgenthau
84. Azizuddin El-Kaissouni, 2002, East Turkistan: China's Forgotten Muslims available at:
https://www.islamawareness.net/Asia/China/cn_article002.html
85. Malkiel, B. & Taylor, P. (2008). *From Wall Street to the Great Wall,* New York: W.W. Norton & Company.

86. *The Investment Cost of the U.S.-China Trade War,* Liberty Street Economics, 28 May 2020, https://libertystreeteconomics.newyorkfed.org/2020/05/the-investment-cost-of-the-us-china-trade-war.html

87. The Message of Imam Khomeini entitled "Outcry of Deliverance", Dhul Hijjah 6, 1408 A.H. published in the Echo of Islam Magazine.

88. Khan, Adnan (2021a) *Strategic Estimate 2021, available at **www.khilafah.com***

89. Saker (2015). The Essential Saker: From The Trenches Of The Emerging Multipolar World United States: Nimble Pluribus The Post-Imperialism Library.

90. Karabell, Z. (2007). People of the Book: The Forgotten History of Islam and the West, London United Kingdom: John Murray

91. Gerber, J. (1992). *The Jews of Spain: A history of the Sephardic Experience,* New York: Free Press.

92. Mayamey, B. (2010). *Zionism: A Critical Account 1897-1948. The Development of Israel and the Exodus of Palestine from A "New Historian"* Perspective POLIS Journal Vol.4, Winter 2010

93. Smith, D.C. (2007) *Palestine and the Arab-Israeli Conflict* (6th Edition). Bedford: St Martins Press.

94. Predecessor of the United Nations

95. Tanner, S. (2004). The Wars of the Bushes: A Father and Son as Military Leaders, USA: Casemate

96. BRI is a transcontinental long-term policy and investment program which aims at infrastructure development and acceleration of the economic

integration of countries along the route of the historic Silk Road. The Initiative was unveiled in 2013 by China's president Xi Jinping and until 2016, was known as OBOR – One Belt One Road. On March 28, 2015, the official outline for the Belt and Road Initiative was issued by the National Development and Reform Commission (NDRC), the Ministry of Foreign Affairs (MOFA) and the Ministry of Commerce (MOFCOM) of the People's Republic of China (PRC), with authorization of the State Council.

97. Harper & Row (1972). *The Limits of Power*, US: Department of State.

98. See Gow, J. (2005). Development theory, Rostow's Five-Stage Model of Development and it Relevance in Globalization, New Castle

99. Washington Consensus, a set of economic policy recommendations for developing countries, and Latin America in particular, that became popular during the 1980s. The term Washington Consensus usually refers to the level of agreement between the IMF, WB, and US Department of the Treasury on those policy recommendations. All shared the view, typically labeled neoliberal, that the operation of the free-market and the reduction of state involvement were crucial to development in the global South.

100. Palley, T. (2001). *Toward a New International Economic Order, Developing World*, Annual Edition, Connecticut: McGraw-Hill.

101. Damao, M. (2018).The Culture of Peace and Development Paradigm in Philippine Context, subscribed from **www.mytuway.wordpress.com**

102. Birdsall, N. (2001). *Life is Unfair: Inequality in the World, Developing World,* Annual Edition, McGraw-Hill, Connecticut.

Part Four
The Post-American World

103. As-Sadr (1982). Our economics, pp. 5-6
104. *Macmillan Dictionary of Modern Economics*, 3rd Ed., 1986, p. 54
105. Fukuyama (1992). *The End of History and the Last Man*, Penguin Publication.

106. Rosen, W. (2007), *Justinian's Flea: Plague, Empire, and the Birth of Europe* Archived 25 January 2010 at the Wayback Machine. Viking Adult, P.3; ISBN 978-0-670-03855-8
107. Wazer, C. (2016). *The Plagues That Might Have Brought down the Roman Empire,* The Atlantic.
108. Cohn, S. (2002). *The Black Death: End of a Paradigm*. American Historical Review, vol.107, 3, pp.703–737
109. Black Death and the Rise of the Ottomans retrieved from **https://www.cambridge.org/core**.
110. Schmidt, S. (2011). To Order the Minds of Scholars: The Discourse of the Peace of Westphalia in

International Relations Literature. *International Studies Quarterly* 55: 601-623

111. Falk, R. (2002). Revisiting Westphalia, Discovering Post-Westphalia, *The Journal of Ethics* 6(4): 311-352.

112. Krasner, S. D. (1999). *Sovereignty: Organized Hypocrisy*. Princeton: Princeton University Press.

113. Keene, E. (2002). *Beyond the Anarchical Society: Grotius, Order, and the Anarchical Society*. Cambridge: Cambridge University Press.

114. Kayaoglu, T. (2010). *Westphalian Eurocentrism in International Relations Theory*, International Studies Review 12: 193-217.

115. Kazemi, B. (2007). A comparison between Western Globalization and Mahdist Globalization. Quarterly Periodical Special Edition Number 2.

116. Giddens, A. (1990). The Consequences of Modernity, London, Polity Press.

117. Castells, M. (1998). The Information Age: Economy, Society and Culture, 3 vols. Oxford: Blackwell.

118. Abdus Salam 2009, pp. 20

119. See the article of Abdus Salam, A. (2009). The Present Economic Crisis: Causes and Effects published by Hizbut Tahrir

120. Daalder I. & Lindsay, J. *Power* and *Cooperation: An American Foreign Policy for the Age of Global Politics*

121. Socialism is a political, social, and economic philosophy encompassing a range of economic and social

systems characterized by social ownership of the means of production and democratic control, such as workers' self-management of enterprises.

122. Costello, L. & Kingston, A. (2020).*The Great Reset Reshaping the Marketing Communications Industry to serve People and Planet*, London **www.purposedisruptors.org**

123. Khan, A. (2020b). *Strategic Estimate 2020,* available at **www.khilafah.com**

124. Global Trends 2025, A transformed world, National Intelligence Council (NIC), 2008

125. The World Health Organization is a specialized agency of the United Nations responsible for international public health. The WHO Constitution states its main objective as the attainment by all peoples of the highest possible level of health.

126. Khan, A. (2021c). Strategic Estimate 2021, Hizbut Tahrir, available at: **www.khilafah.com**

127. A new Bretton Woods moment**https://www.imf.org/en/News/Articles/2020/10/15/sp101520-a-new-bretton-woods-moment**

128. Now is the time for a 'great reset,' Klaus Schwab, World Economic Forum (WEF), 3 June 2020, **https://www.weforum.org/agenda/2020/06/now-is-the-time-for-a-great-reset/** Coronavirus crisis presents a 'golden opportunity' to reboot the

economy, Prince Charles says, CNBC, 3 June 2020, **https://www.cnbc.com/2020/06/03/prince-charles-covid-19-a-golden-opportunity-to-reboot-the-economy.html**

129. Strategic Estimate 2021
130. Roth, S. (2021). *The Great Reset of Management and Organization Theory*, A European perspective, European Management Journal, La Rochelle Business School **https://www.researchgate.net/publication/351995271**
131. Nair, C. (2021) The Great Reset, SID Directors Bulletin 2021
132. Understanding The Great Reset: an interview with Richard Florida by Ontario Business Report in 2021
133. Lachmann, R. (2011). *The roots of American Decline* pp. 44-49, New York
134. Zack, N. (2020). *The American Tragedy of COVID-19 Social and Political Crises of 2020.*
135. Hobson, C. (2021) *The Pandemic and our Place in the World* available at **https://www.e-ir.info/2021/03/03/the-pandemic-and-our-place-in-the-world/**
136. Harmes, A. (2001), 'Institutional investors and Polanyi's double movement: a model of contemporary currency crises', Review of International Political Economy, 8:3, p. 389-437.

137. Lagna, A. (2012). *The IMF and American Power,* available at: **https://www.e-ir.info/2012/08/09/the-imf-and-american-power/**
138. Strongin, S. & Mirabal, D. (2020). *The Great Reset a Framework for Investing After COVID-19*, The Goldman Sachs Group, Inc.
139. Heine, J. (2020). *A World Order Turned Upside Down, A world Before and After Covid-19*, Stockholm: European Institute of International Studies
140. Stuenkel, O. (2020). *Post-western World and the Rise of Parallel Order'*, The Diplomat, archived **http://thediplomat.com/2006/09/the-post-western-world-and-the-rise-of-a-parallel-order/**
141. Riordan, S. (2020). *Covid-19 and the Digitalization of Diplomacy, A world Before and After Covid-19*, Stockholm: European Institute of International Studies.
142. Levent Uzun, L. (2015). *The Digital World and the Elements in Digital Communication and FL Learning Uludag University, Turkey* DOI: 10.4018/978-1-4666-5888-2.ch203
143. Damao, 2021, the journal is entitled: The Modular Classes During Covid-19 Pandemic: The Emerging Opportunities, Challenges and Difficulties published by International Journal for Research Publications published in 2021
144. MENA ECONOMIC UPDATE OCTOBER 2020, *Trading Together: Reviving Middle East and North Africa Regional Integration in the Post-Covid Era,* Washington DC: World Bank.

145. Khan, Adnan (2021c) *Strategic Estimate 2021, available at* **www.khilafah.com**

146. Stevens, E. (2002). *Electronic Money and the Future of Central Banks*, Federal Reserve Bank of Cleveland Research Department: ISSN 0428-1276

147. Guttmann, R. (2002) Cybercash: *The Coming Era of Electronic Money* Palgrafe Macmillan pp. 9

148. Neda, P. (2014) : *The use of electronic money and its impact on monetary policy, Journal of Contemporary Economic and Business Issues*, ISSN 1857-9108, Ss. Cyril and Methodius University in Skopje, Faculty of Economics, Skopje, Vol. 1, Issue. 2, pp. 79-92

149. Friedman, H. H., & Friedman, L. W. (2009). *The Global Financial Crisis of 2008: What Went Wrong?* (SSRN Scholarly Paper No. ID 1356193)

150. Harde, W., Harvey, C. & Reule, R. (2019). Understanding Cryptocurrencies, Germany: International Research Training Group 1792, Available at: **http://irtg1792.hu-berlin.de**: ISSN 2568-5619

151. GlobalFindex. 2017. \The Global Findex Database 2017." The World Bank. Retrieved on the 05.06.2018 from https://globalfindex.worldbank.org

152. CPMI, (2016). Statistics on payment, clearing and settlement systems in the CPMI countries Figures for 2015. Technicalreport, Bank for International Settlements. Committee on Payments and Market Infrastructures. **http://www.bis.org/cpmi/publ/d152.htm.**

Accessed 01 Jan 2018; CPSS, (2012). Statistics on payment, clearing and settlement systems in the CPSS countries - Figures for 2010. Technical report, Bank of International Settlements. Committee on Payment and Settlement Systems.
http://www.bis.org/cpmi/publ/d99.htm. Accessed 01 Jan 2018

153. Reiss, D. (2018) *Is money going digital? An alternative perspective on the current hype* **https://doi.org/10.1186/s40854-018-0097-x** Reiss Financial Innovation (2018) 4:14

154. Hofman, A. (2014). *The Dawn of the National Currency – An Exploration of Country-Based Cryptocurrencies.* Available at: Bitcoin Magazine Website: **https://bitcoinmagazine.com/articles/dawnnational-currency-exploration-country-based-cryptocurrencies-1394146138**

155. IRENA (2017), Electric Vehicles: technology brief, Abu Dhabi: International Renewable Energy Agency.

156. "Electric Cars @ProjectDrawdown #ClimateSolutions" (**https://www.drawdown.org/solutions/electriccars**) Project Drawdown. 6 February 2020. Archived (**https://web.archive.org/web/20201127115601**/https://www.drawdown.org/solutions/electric-cars) from the original on 27 November 2020. Retrieved 20 November 2020.

157. Le Petit, Yoann. "Electric vehicle life cycle analysis and raw material availability" (**https://www.transpor**tenvironment.org/sites/te/files/publications/2017_10_EV_LCA_briefing_final.pdf) (PDF). transportenvironment.org Transport & Environment. Archived (**https://web.archive.org/web/2021040** 4030406/https://www.transportenvironment.org/sites/te/files/publications/2017_10_EV_LCA_briefing final.pdf) (PDF) from the original on 4 April 2021. Retrieved 9 February 2021.

158. "Move to net zero 'inevitably means more mining' " (**https://www.bbc.com/news/science** environment- 57234610) . BBC News. 24 May 2021. Archived (**https://web.archive.org/web/20210604073918/ https://www.bbc.com/news/sc** ence-environment-57234610) from the original on 4 June 2021. Retrieved 4 June 2021.

159. Harvard Kennedy School, Belfer Center for Science and International Affairs. (2011, July). *Will Electric Cars Transform the U.S. Car Market?* Cambridge: Lee, H. & Lovellette, G. Retrieved from http://belfercenter.ksg.harvard.edu/files/Lee%20Lovellette%20Electric%20Vehicles%20DP%202011%20web.pdf

160. Oil 2021: Analysis and forecast to 2026, IEA Publications International Energy Agency, see **www.iea.org**

161. Watson, A. (2020). *'Questions for the Integrated Review #2: How to Engage: Deep and Narrow or Wide and Shallow?'* Oxford Research Group. 14 July. **https://www.oxfordresearchgroup.org.uk/questions-for-the-integrated-review-2-how-to-engage-deep-and-narrow-or-wide-and-shallow**

162. Khan, Adnan (2021d) *Strategic Estimate 2021, available at* **www.khilafah.com**

163. "Working Together to Deliver a Brighter Future for Belt and Road Cooperation," *The Second Belt and Road Forum for International Cooperation*, April 26, 2019, http://www.beltandroadforum.org/english/n100/2019/0426/c22-1266.html.

164. "Full Text of the Vision for Maritime Cooperation under the Belt and Road Initiative," The State Council of the People's Republic of China, June 20, 2017, **http://english.www.gov.cn/archive/publications/2017/06/20/** content_281475691873460.htm.

165. Russel, D. & Berger, B. (2020). Weaponizing the Belt and Road Initiative. New York: A Report of the Asia Society Policy Institute

166. Kirk Lancaster and Michael Rubin, "Assessing the Early Response to Beijing's Pandemic Diplomacy," Council on Foreign Relations, April 30, 2020, **https://www.cfr.org/blog/assessing-early-response-beijings-pandemic-diplomacy**.

167. "China's Medical Expert Team Arrives in Philippines to Help Fight COVID-19," *Xinhua*, April 5, 2020, **http://www.xinhuanet.** com/english/2020-04/05/c_138949480.htm; "China Donates Additional 20,000 COVID-19 Fast Test Kits to Cambodia," *Xinhua*, March 28, 2020, http://www.xinhuanet.com/english/2020-03/28/c_138925498.htm; "Chinese Foundations Donate to Myanmar in Fight against COVID-19," Xinhua, March 30, 2020, **http://www.xinhuanet.com/english/2020-**03/30/c_138931143.htm.

168. Meera Srinivasan, "China to Extend $500mn 'Assistance' to Sri Lanka," *The Hindu*, March 18, 2020, **https://www.thehindu**.com/news/international/china-to-extend-500mn-assistance-to-sri-lanka/article31101962.ece;

169. "Sri Lanka Receives Chinese Medical Supplies to Combat COVID-19," Xinhua, April 2, 2020,

http://www.xinhuanet.com/ english/2020-04/02/c_138941365.htm.

170. Kirk Lancaster and Michael Rubin, "Assessing the Early Response to Beijing's Pandemic Diplomacy," Council on Foreign Relations, April 30, 2020, **https://www.cfr.org/blog/assessing-early-response-**beijings-pandemic-diplomacy; "Cambodian PM Says Joint COVID-19 Fight Uplifts Cambodia-China Ties," *Global Times*, April 8, 2020, https://www.globaltimes.cn/content/1184967.shtml.

171. Nasr, 2003, p.96

172. Qur'an 30:41

173. Intergovernmental Panel on Climate Change, 2001: The Scientific bases

174. Met Office, 2005, p.40

175. See Khan, A. (2008) Geopolitical Myth. Hizbut Tahrir

176. Ouis, S. "Global Environmental Relations: An Islamic Perspective" No Date.<http://www.aml.org.uk/journal/4.1/SPO%20-%20Global%20Environment%20Relations.pdf#search=%22soumaya%20pernilla%22> (8 Aug. 2006).

177. UNEP, (2010), 2 Syntheses for Policy Makers, p. 1

178. See electronic Journal pubished in December 2012 titled, "A Model of Green Economy for Developing Countries" Electronic copy available at: **http://ssrn.com/abstract=2192369**

179. GREEN ECONOMY IN ACTION: Articles and Excerpts that Illustrate Green Economy and Sustainable Development Efforts. August 2012

180. Walsh, J.E. 2013. Melting ice: What is happening to Arctic sea ice, and what does it mean for us? *Oceanography* 26(2):171–181, http://dx.doi.org/10.5670/oceanog.2013.19.

181. See The Environmental Problem Its Causes & Islam's Solution published by Hizb ut-Tahrir – Denmark 1430 A.H. / 2009 A.D.

182. Steven Kenney & Ross Harrison Middle East Conflict and Covid-19 — A View from 2025, Mei Strategic Foresight Initiative June 2020 Policy Paper

183. Ibid

184. Phillips, C. & Valbjorn, M. 'What is in a Name?': The Role of (Different) Identities in the Multiple Proxy Wars in Syria', *Small Wars & Insurgencies* 29 (3), 414-433

185. Terril, W. (2011). THE SAUDI-IRANIAN RIVALRY AND THE FUTURE OF MIDDLE EAST SECURITY, United States: Strategic Studies Institute (SSI) Available at: http://www.StrategicStudiesInstitute.army.mil/

186. "Iraqi President calls for strategic ties with Iran," Kuwait News Agency, March 28, 2011.

187. Saudi Arabia and Iran: The Struggle to Shape the Middle East Published by The Foreign Policy Centre (FPC Think Tank Ltd)

188. Kristian Coates Ulrichsen, "Israel and the Arab Gulf States: Drivers and Directions of Change," Rice University's Baker Institute for Policy, September 2016, 3–4, https://www.bakerinstitute.org/media/files/research_document/13eaaa71/CME-pub-GCCIsrael-090716. pdf; Simon Henderson, "Israeli-GCC Ties Twenty-Five Years After the First Gulf War," The Washington Institute for Near East Policy, in Focus Quarterly Policy Analysis, October 14, 2015, www.washingtoninstitute.org/policy-analysis/view/israel-gcc-ties-twenty-five-years-after-the-first-gulf-war.

189. Ulrichsen, "Israel and the Arab Gulf States," 2, 6–9; Asher Orkaby, "Rivals with Benefits: Israel and Saudi Arabia's Secret History of Cooperation," *Foreign Affairs*, March 13, 2015, www.foreignaffairs.com/articles/middle-east/2015-03-13/rivals-benefits.

190. Hussein Ibish, "After the UAE, Who Will and Won't Be Next to Normalize With Israel?," The Arab Gulf States Institute in Washington (AGSIW) (blog), August 24, 2020, https://agsiw.org/after-the-uae-who-will-and-wont-be-next-to-normalize-with-israel/.

191. Robert F. Worth, "Mohammed bin Zayed's Dark Vision of the Middle East's Future," *The New York Times Magazine*, January 9, 2020, www.nytimes.com/2020/01/09/magazine/united-arab-emirates-mohammed-bin-zayed.html
192. Khan, 2008, Geopolitical Myth: Dubai presents a new Economic Model for the Muslim World, p. 60
193. Hosein, I. (2017) DAJJĀL, THE QUR'ĀN AND AWWAL AL-ZAMĀN, Tobago and Trinidad: Imran N. Hosein Publications

Bibliography

Abdus Salam, A. (2009). *The Present Economic Crisis: Causes and Effects: Towards a Tranquil Safe World under the Shade of the Economic System of Islam*, Sudan: Hizb ut Tahrir

Armstrong, K. (2002). *Islam: A short History.* New York: the Modern Library.

Ashford, E. (2020). *The Aftermath: American Power after COVID-19.* Rome, Italy, Istituto Affari Internazionali (IAI)

As-Sad'r, M. (1982). *Iqtisaduna: Our Economics.* Vol. 1, Part 2, Tehran: world Organization For Islamic services.

As-Sallabi, A. (2007). *Umar Ibn Al-Khattab: His Life and Times*, Riyadh, Saudi Arabia: International Islamic Publishing House.

Betts, R. (2010). *Conflict or Cooperation: Three Visions Revisited*,
United States: Columbia University.

Bilgrin, P. (2012). *Civilization, Dialogue, Security: The Challenge Of Post-Secularism And The Limits Of Civilizational Dialogue, British International Studies Association*, Available at: Review of International Studies (2012), 38, 1099–1115
doi:10.1017/S0260210512000496

Birdsall, N. (2001). *Life is Unfair: Inequality in the World*,

Developing World, Annual Edition, Connecticut: McGraw-Hill.

Brown, S. (1991). *Explaining the Transformation of World Politics,*
International Journal 46, No. 2, pp. 207-219

Castells, M. (1998). *The Information Age: Economy, Society and Culture*, 3 vols. Oxford: Blackwell.

Costello, L. & Kingston, A. (2020).*The Great Reset Reshaping the Marketing Communications Industry to serve People and Planet*, London www.purposedisruptors.org

Cox, M. (2003) 'The Empire's Back in Town: Or America's Imperial Temptation – Again', Millennium, 32 (1), 1–27

Curtis, M. (2008).*The Great Political Theories, Vol. 2,* New York: Harperperrenial, Publishers.

Damao, M. (2015). *The Comprehensive Agreement on the Bangsamoro: A Stakeholders' Analysis*, Cotabato City: Notre Dame Press.

Damao, M. (2021). *The Evolutionary Responsefor Bangsamoro Self-Rule. International Journal of Arts, Humanities and Social Studies*, 3(5), 01-08.

Devries, P. (2016). *An Analysis of Crypto-currency, Bitcoin, and the Future*, University of Houston – Downtown Article ·

Entessar, N. (1992). *Kurdish Ethnonationalism,* London: Lynne

Rienner Publishers.

Falk, R. (2002). *Revisiting Westphalia, Discovering Post-Westphalia,* The Journal of Ethics 6(4): 311-352.

Friedman, H. & Friedman, L. (2009). *The Global Financial Crisis of 2008: What Went Wrong?* SSRN Scholarly Paper No. ID 1356193

Gardini, G.L. 2020. *The world before and after Covid19: Intellectual Reflections on Politics, Diplomacy and International Relations*, European Institute of International Studies Press, Salamanca, Stockholm

Gerber, J. (1992). *The Jews of Spain: A history of the Sephardic Experience*, New York: Free Press.

Giddens, A. (1990). *The Consequences of Modernity*. London, Polity Press.

Harde, W., Harvey, C. & Reule, R. (2019). *Understanding Crypto-currencies,* Germany: International Research Training Group 1792, Available at: http://irtg1792.hu-berlin.de**:** ISSN 2568-5619

Harper & Row (1972). *The Limits of Power*, US: Department of State.

Heine, J. (2020). *A World Order Turned Upside Down, A world Before and After Covid-19*, Stockholm: European Institute of International Studies.

Hosein, I. (2017) *DAJJĀL, THE QUR'ĀN AND AWWAL AL-ZAMĀN*, Tobago and Trinidad: Imran N. Hosein Publications

Ibn Khaldun (1969). Dawood, NJ (ed). *Muqaddimah: An Introduction to History*, Princeton University Press, ISBN 9780691099460

Ikenberry, J. (2005). *Power and liberal order: America's postwar world order in transition, International Relations of the Asia-Pacific* Volume 5 (2005) 133–152, Bendheim Hall, Woodrow Wilson School, Princeton: Princeton University.

Ikenberry J., Mastanduno, M. & Wohlforth, W. (2009). *Introduction Unipolarity, State Behavior, and Systemic Consequences, World Politics,* Volume 61, Number 1, January 2009, pp. 1-27 (Article), Cambridge University Press
IPCC (2001). *Climate Change 2001: The Scientific* Basis, Cambridge: University Press.

James, H. (2006) *The Roman Predicament: How the Rules of International Order Create the Politics of Empire*. Princeton NJ: Princeton University Press.

Jannace, W. & Tiffany, P. (2019). *A New World Order: The Rule of Law, or the Law of Rulers?* Fordham International Law Journal, 42 (5), 2

Karabell, Z. (2007). *People of the Book: The Forgotten History of Islam and the West,* London United Kingdom: John Murray.

Kayaoglu, T. (2010). *Westphalian Eurocentrism in International Relations Theory*. International Studies Review 12: 193 217.

Kazemi, B. (2007). *A comparison between Western Globalization and Mahdist Globalization*. Quarterly Periodical Special Edition Number 2.

Keddie, N. (1972). Sayyid Jamal Ad-din Al-Afghani: A Politcal Biography, Berkeley

Keene, E. (2002). *Beyond the Anarchical Society: Grotius, Order, and the Anarchical Society*. Cambridge: Cambridge University Press.

Kenney, S. & Harrison, R. (2020). Middle East Conflict and Covid-19: A View from 2025, Mei Strategic Foresight Initiative June 2020 Policy Paper

Krasner, S. D. (1999). *Sovereignty: Organized Hypocrisy*. Princeton: Princeton University Press.

Krastev, I. & Leonard, M. (2021).*The Crisis of American Power: How Europeans See Biden's America,* European Council on Foreign Relations

Lari, M. (2006).*Western Civilization Through Muslim Eyes.* IRI: Foundation of Islamic Cultural Propagation

Malkiel, B. & Taylor, P. (2008) *From Wall Street to the Great Wall,* New York: W.W. Norton & Company.

Mayamey, B. (2010). *Zionism: A Critical Account 1897-1948. The Development of Israel and the Exodus of Palestine from A "New Historian"* Perspective POLIS Journal Vol.4, Winter 2010

Met office (2005). Climate Change and the Greenhouse Effect, Exeter: The Met Office.

Mishra, P. (2012). From the Ruins of Empire: The Revolt against the West and the Remaking of Asia, United States: Farrar, Strauss and Giroux.

Morgenthau, H. (2006). *Politics Among Nations*. New York: McGraw-Hill.

Muhammadi, M. (2006). *Islamic Revolution and the World System: Imam Khomeini and the International System*, IRI: International affairs Department.

Nasr, S. (2003). '*Islam, the Contemporary Islamic World, and the Environmental Crisis' in*: Foltz, R., Denny, F., Baharuddin, A. (ed) Islam and Ecology: A Bestowed Trust, Cambridge, Massachusetts: Harvard University Press, pp 85-105

Neda, P. (2014). *The use of electronic money and its impact on monetary policy*, Journal of Contemporary Economic and Business Issues, ISSN 1857-9108, Ss. Cyril and Methodius University in Skopje, Faculty of Economics, Skopje, Vol. 1, Issue. 2, pp. 79-92

Palley, T. (2001) *Toward a New International Economic Order, Developing World*, Annual Edition, Connecticut: McGraw-Hill.

Pishva'I, M. (2007) *History of Islam up to the Demise of the Prophet,* Qum: E'timad Press.

Porter, P. (2013). *Sharing Power? Prospects for A U.S. Concert-Balance Strategy,* US: Strategic Studies Institute.

Quinn, A. & Kitchen, N (2019) *Understanding American Power: Conceptual Clarity, Strategic Priorities, and the Decline Debate*, Vol. 10, Issue1,US: Global Policy Durham University and John Wiley & Sons Ltd.

Qur'an, The translations used in this paper are from Abdullah Yusuf Ali (2003), *The Meaning of the Holy Qur'an,* Maryland: Amana Publications.

Riordan, S. (2020) *Covid-19 and the Digitalization of Diplomacy, A world Before and After Covid-19*, Stockholm: European Institute of International Studies.

Roth, S. (2021).*The Great Reset of Management and Organization Theory.* A European perspective, European Management Journal, La Rochelle Business School
https://www.researchgate.net/publication/351995271

Saker (2015). *The Essential Saker: From the Trenches Of The Emerging Multipolar World United States*: Nimble Pluribus the Post-Imperialism Library

Schmidt, S. (2011). *To Order the Minds of Scholars: The*

Discourse of the Peace of Westphalia in International Relations Literature, International Studies Quarterly 55: 601-623

Schwartz, S. (2003). *The Two Faces of Islam*, New York: Random House, Inc.

Smith, D.C. (2007). *Palestine and the Arab-Israeli Conflict* (6th Edition). Bedford: St Martins Press.

Stevens, E. (2002). *Electronic Money and the Future of Central Banks,* Federal Reserve Bank of Cleveland Research Department: ISSN 0428-1276

Strongin, S. & Mirabal, D. (2020). *The Great Reset a Framework for Investing After COVID-19*, The Goldman Sachs Group, Inc.

Tanner, S. (2004). *The Wars of the Bushes: A Father and Son as Military Leaders*, USA: Casemate

Uli, S. (2004). *The Rise of the Ottoman Empire: The Black Death in medieval Anatolia and its impact on Turkish civilization,* in Neguin Yavari et al., eds., Views from the Edge: Essays in Honor of Richard W. Bulliet (New York : Columbia University Press 2004), 270 –2 .

Walsh, J.E. 2013. *Melting ice: What is happening to Arctic sea ice, and what does it mean for us? Oceanography* 26(2):171–181

Waltz, K. (1979). *Theory of International Politics,* Mass: Addison-Wesley

Wazer, C. (2016). *The Plagues That Might Have Brought down the Roman Empire,* The Atlantic.

Wohlforth, W. (1999). *The Stability of a Unipolar World, The MIT Press Journals, International Security,* Vol. 24, No. 1, pp. 5-41

Yazdi, M. (2011). Islamic Political Theory (Legislation), IRI: ABWA.

Zakaria, F. (2008). *The Future of American Power: How America Can Survive the Rise of the Rest,* US: From Foreign Affairs, Council on Foreign Relations.

Zala, B. (2013). *Rethinking Polarity for the Twenty-first Century: Perceptions of Order in International Society*, Birmingham: University of Birmingham.

Acknowledgment

Like all other books, this would not have written without the support and inspiration of friends and colleagues. My passion for this subject goes back from my high school years. I love reading world history and Islamic history in particular. Being a member of organization advancing the cause of the Bangsamoro, I attended to many lectures and Islamic symposia discussing the plight of the Muslims. In my college days, internet emerged. Internet helped me connect with different international scholars and analysts around the world. I had also studied in local Madrasa (school), which helped me familiarize with the Noble Quran and the prophetic traditions.

The main reason why I wrote this book is that I want to present an alternative perspective given that there are various conflicting views on Islam and the problem the Ummah is in. The divide in the world of Islam is so deep and that they became pawns of Great Powers pitting against one another. I and MB had the same beliefs that mankind is now living in a transition period before the rise of Israel in the center-stage. May this book shed light to the real problem besetting the Ummah.

I thank my friend A.S.A. for his full review and feedback. I hope this book makes a contribution for the betterment of Ummah.

About The Author

The author is an analyst, consultant, and peace and justice advocate and a content writer. His interest is on economy, politics, history, international relations, governance and peace and development. Considering the ideological confusion of the Ummah today, which leads Muslims into the downward spiral of violence, conflict and corruption, there is a need to write an alternative view that gives analysis and clarifies complex political situations, thus presenting more balanced perspectives.

The author was born in Tugal, Midsayap in 1989. Having completed his primary and secondary education, he then studied Bachelor of Science in Secondary Education major in English language and literature at Notre Dame of Midsayap College. He finished a short course on public policy development and advocacy in the University of the Philippines, Quezon City, the most prestigious school in the Philippines. He was also an intern at the House of Representatives in 2011 in the office of the Deputy Speaker for Mindanao, Hon. Maria Isabelle Climaco.

He completed his master's degree in Peace and Development in the prominent school of Mindanao, Notre Dame University, Cotabato City in 2015 with a thesis entitled, "The Comprehensive Agreement of the Bangsamoro: A Stakeholders' Analysis." He finished his PhD in Peace and Development in Cotabato State University, Cotabato City in 2020 with a dissertation entitled, "Promotion of Peace and Development in Bangsamoro Areas: The Case of the Contribution of JICA Comprehensive Capacity Development Project."

He is a Chief Executive Officer of the Bangsamoro Dialogue for Peace and Justice, Inc. It is an independent non-governmental organization organized to render service to the local communities in the Bangsamoro areas.

Printed in Great Britain
by Amazon